Raising an Optimistic Child

A Proven Plan for Depression-Proofing Young Children—for Life

BOB MURRAY, Ph.D., and ALICIA FORTINBERRY

McGraw·Hill

New York   Chicago   San Francisco   Lisbon   London   Madrid   Mexico City
Milan   New Delhi   San Juan   Seoul   Singapore   Sydney   Toronto

Library of Congress Cataloging-in-Publication Data

Murray, Bob.
    Raising an optimistic child : a proven plan for depression-proofing young children—for life / Bob Murray, Alicia Fortinberry.
       p.   cm.
    Includes bibliographical references and index.
    ISBN 0-07-145948-0
       1. Child psychology.   2. Depression in children—Popular works.   3. Child rearing—Psychological aspects.   4. Parenting—Psychological aspects.   5. Optimism.
    I. Fortinberry, Alicia.   II. Title.

    HQ772.M88   2006
    618.92'89—dc22
                                         2005030235

2 3 4 5 6 7 8 9 0   FGR/FGR   0 9 8 7 6

ISBN 0-07-145948-0

McGraw-Hill books are available at special quantity discounts to use as premiums and sales promotions, or for use in corporate training programs. For more information, please write to the Director of Special Sales, Professional Publishing, McGraw-Hill, Two Penn Plaza, New York, NY 10121-2298. Or contact your local bookstore.

This book is printed on acid-free paper.

CONTENTS

◉

PART I

UNDERSTANDING AND PREVENTING DEPRESSION IN CHILDREN

PART II

SEVEN STEPS TO DEPRESSION-PROOF YOUR CHILD—FOR LIFE

PART III

APPLYING OPTIMISTIC PARENTING STRATEGIES TO
COMMON CHALLENGES

ACKNOWLEDGMENTS

◉

Our enormous gratitude to our invaluable long-term collaborator, Sophie Ozolins. We are delighted to work again with our perceptive and encouraging editor, Judith McCarthy, and members of the McGraw-Hill team including Nancy Hall, our project editor, and Lizz Aviles, our senior publicist. As always, thanks also to our agent, Jeanne Fredericks, for her thoughtful and sensitive support.

INTRODUCTION

◉

The elements that enable us to be optimistic and experience authentic life-long happiness, true friendships, and fulfillment are largely set in place by age six. And so are the conditions for depression, anxiety, and many physical illnesses, from heart disease to diabetes.

Yet there is little information for parents of very young kids on how to create the conditions that will foster ongoing optimism and prevent depression. This is partly because for the past decade or so the mainstream techniques for preventing and treating mood disorders have involved changing how you think about things, yet a thought-based, or "cognitive," approach doesn't work for young children who can't analyze their own thoughts. Cognitive psychology has limitations for adults as well, since research now shows that our emotions and the state of our relationships determine our thoughts and self-esteem, rather than the other way around. In fact, overlaying negative thoughts with positive ones may just suppress them temporarily.

Particularly up to age six, children take their thinking and emotional cues from you and the other adults in their immediate environment (including older siblings). Your child's brain is a recorder that will faithfully store every nuance of adult interaction with each other and herself for duplication in later life. In fact, even the structure and functions of her brain will be shaped by these interactions. If her early relationships are positive and affirming, she will not only feel safe and loved now but will create affirming relationships and experience well-being later in life. If her early relationships are fractured, these conflicts and tensions also will be almost uncannily reproduced as she gets older. The result: a child who feels overwhelmed, helpless, and hopeless—perhaps even depressed and anxious—and an adult who tends to search out relationships that ferment anxiety and depression.

During the past few decades, academics have heatedly debated whether the prime determinant of optimism, pessimism, and depression is nature or nurture, or, more recently, a combination. In 2005, researchers at the University of Queensland, Australia, were surprised when their study suggested that a child's biology played a larger than expected role.[1] However, the vast preponderance of evidence cites a delicate dance between genetics and a child's environment as the ultimate deciding factor. The most important element in that environment is the parents' relationship and their parenting styles.

As a psychologist (Bob) and a psychotherapist (Alicia) as well as teachers and organizational consultants (both of us), for more than two decades we have helped individuals, families, and organizations to create optimism and strong, supportive relationships that promote success in all areas of life. Our highly successful international Uplift Program and books, including *Creating Optimism: A Proven Seven-Step Program for Overcoming Depression*, have given thousands of people practical, simple tools to prevent and overcome mood disorders and discover authentic happiness.

Many parents and health professionals have asked us to expand on the information in *Creating Optimism* regarding how to create strong, harmonious families that stimulate the innate capacity of young children for optimism and resilience.

Recent research in the fields of neurobiology, movement physiology, and attachment theory has shed new light on preventing mood disorders in early childhood. At the same time, new wisdom is emerging from an unexpected source—the distant past of our hunter-gatherer ancestors. Drawing on these resources as well as our clinical experience, we'll share our step-by-step process for creating an optimistic and depression-free family. This book offers a concrete blueprint for creating an environment for the child that will ensure her ability to deal with whatever challenges our increasingly troubled world offers. It will help guarantee that the child never has to face these challenges without support, encouragement, and strong inner values.

In Part I we explain the conditions for optimism and emotional health and help you understand how depression and behavioral problems can get a foothold in the early years.

Part II provides our practical, seven-step plan for depression-proofing your child for life:

Step 1: Don't let your inner saboteur affect your family—identify and change negative parenting patterns.

Step 2: Determine a healthy balance between work and family—establish a Parenting Priority Plan, and stick to it.

Step 3: Build a nexus of supportive relationships around yourself and your child—using our Needs-Based Dialogue techniques.

Step 4: Set up a clear process for family decision-making—even young children can learn these skills at the Family Powwow.

Step 5: Establish rules, roles, and rituals—the essential ingredients of a harmonious family.

Step 6: Create a family culture of appropriate praise—how to nurture healthy self-esteem and competence.

Step 7: Develop and nurture shared values and beliefs—for family bonding, resilience, and empowerment.

Part III focuses on how to successfully deal with common parenting challenges, including combating your own depression; enhancing competence and mastery for lifelong optimism; dealing with attention deficit disorders (ADD/ADHD); improving body image; mitigating the effects of separation, divorce, and loss; nurturing togetherness for single parents and blended families; and protecting your young child from bullying and potentially harmful and depressing outside influences.

Authors' Note

◉

We address our readers as parents but are also speaking to all those who care about the welfare of young children and the adults they will become. The techniques outlined in this book are designed for families with children under age six, but most are applicable, and just as effective, for older kids. For clarity, we have chosen to alternate the pronouns *he* and *she* in consecutive chapters. Although we do not assume that the mother is always the child's primary caregiver, for simplicity we often use the term *mother* to stand in for the primary caregiver.

PART I

UNDERSTANDING AND PREVENTING DEPRESSION IN CHILDREN

1

THE KEY TO PARENTING AN OPTIMISTIC CHILD

◉

E mma, usually a lively, healthy, and inquisitive four-year-old who enjoyed play dates and games, became increasingly lethargic, obstinate, and uncommunicative. Her mother, Laura, grew concerned when Emma continued to have trouble sleeping. She also stopped wanting to play with her friends or go to preschool or even roughhouse with her dad, and she complained of constant stomachaches. When Emma's pediatrician couldn't find a physical cause for the problems, he suggested putting Emma on antidepressants.

Laura, who was concerned about the use of drugs not proven for young children, contacted Bob. "I'm frantic and confused," she told him. "Nothing seems to work, and I just get more frustrated and less patient and able to cope."

"Tell me about what's been happening at home," he suggested.

"Things haven't been great," Laura admitted. "My husband, Julian, has been under enormous pressure at work over the past year, and we seem to fight all the time. I've been worried about what would happen if Julian loses his job, trying to save every penny, and at the same time terrified that the relationship might fall apart. Come to think of it, we've both been upset and distracted around Emma, and maybe she's reacting to that."

"Let's work on improving how you and Julian get along and handle stress," suggested Bob. "I can also recommend some simple parenting principles that might help." Four months later, the couple's relationship had vastly improved, allowing them to support each other through a difficult time and also to focus more on Emma's needs.

Raising an optimistic, emotionally healthy child isn't easy in today's stressful world. By attending to the factors in Emma's environment that were setting her up for depression and following some practical parenting guidelines, her parents not only enormously increased their young child's well-being but also established the groundwork for her lifelong optimism and resilience.

THE DEPRESSION EPIDEMIC

Similar to Emma, more and more young children are being diagnosed with depression and related disorders, such as anxiety and posttraumatic stress disorder (PTSD),[1] as early as age one (or even birth).

In its 2001 report "Depression in Children and Adolescents," the National Institute of Mental Health (NIMH) stated that one in three American children suffers from depression, and 4 percent of children under age six—more than a million—are diagnosed as depressed. More recent studies show that the real number is probably much higher and, according to a recent Harvard study, rising at a rate of 23 percent a year. Alarmingly, preschoolers are the fastest growing market for antidepressants,[2] despite government warnings of possible dangers[3] and the fact that, according to the Food and Drug Administration (FDA), antidepressants probably don't work for kids anyway.[4]

However, a far greater problem is the many more children who may not display depression symptoms but who are experiencing events in their crucial first six years that will lead to emotional problems later on. As children reach adolescence and move on to college, more than 60 percent will suffer bouts of severe depression.[5] According to NIMH, suicide is now the third most frequent cause of teenage death. A 2001 report by the World Health Organization states that by the time your young child is a teenager, depression will be the number-two killer in the world (second only to heart disease, to which depression is a contributory factor). Even the depression that is increasingly affecting the elderly can have its origins in very early life.[6]

DEPRESSION AND ANXIETY IN THE MODERN FAMILY

At the heart of the depression epidemic is the enormous pressure our modern lifestyle places on the unsupported and increasingly fragmented family, commercial interests that target even younger "consumers," and a deteriorating social and ecological environment. All of these can create trauma in young children, deprive them of their emotional needs, and strip them of their innate optimism.

It's difficult to raise your child to be confident, purposeful, emotionally healthy, and optimistic if you're worried about developing your career (or just keeping your job), paying bills, maintaining a good relationship with your partner, eating right and exercising, and meeting the countless responsibilities of modern life. There just never seems to be enough time. The situation is made worse if you've also lost many traditional sources of support, such as helpful relatives living nearby, a close-knit neighborhood, or understanding physicians and clergy with sufficient time to listen to your problems and proffer unbiased advice. It's even harder for isolated single parents or conflict-ridden blended families.

Familial stresses and their effects on the child are far more potent risk factors for depression than individual genetic predisposition, although these environmental factors can turn the gene for depression on—or off. In fact, your child can become depressed without ever having that gene, or be depression-free even if he does.

Taking control of your own emotional life is the best thing you can do to ensure your child's emotional health.[7] Twenty-five to 30 percent of women suffer from depression, and children of depressed parents have a 40 percent chance of developing depression themselves, as compared to 20 percent for the population as a whole (male and female).[8] While being depressed and anxious doesn't necessarily make you a bad parent or condemn your child to a mood disorder, it is important that you seek help. The more optimistic you become, the more your child's natural optimism can come to the fore.

AT ODDS WITH OUR GENES

As far as paleontologists and anthropologists can tell, long-lasting clinical depression did not exist among our hunter-gatherer ancestors. In fact, according to biopsychologist Bjørn Grinde, humans are innately optimistic "because a good mood, and to some extent a rose-colored view of the world, is to the genes' advantage."[9] Faith in a positive outcome, each other, and the gods gave early humans the determination and resilience to endure difficult conditions such as drought until the rains came.

However, the mismatch between how we live and how we were genetically designed to function threatens to turn off our species' inbuilt genetic predisposition for optimism and create a pessimistic society.[10] We are, as Grinde says, a "Stone Age creature in a Jet Age zoo."[11]

The advent of farming, which replaced the hunter-gatherer lifestyle anywhere from five to ten thousand years ago, altered, for the worse, the way we relate to each other and to our environment. The hunter-gatherer band fully supported both parents and children, who were valued by the entire tribe and, to a large extent, raised communally. A young mother needs other women around much of the time to share the burden, take her child when she's weary, give advice, and lend emotional support. Day care and the occasional mothers' group meeting are not adequate substitutes. A father of a young child also needs the advice, company, and backup of other men.

In humans the art of parenting, like so many other things, is learned, not instinctual. Unlike a kangaroo or mountain goat, you weren't born knowing how to parent effectively. Through what writer and biologist Matt Ridley calls "nature *via* nurture," nature equips us with genes that predispose us to learn by experience.[12] Today, as in ancient times, child rearing is a skill acquired largely by observation. A hunter-gatherer girl learned mothering from observing all the other women in the tribe and by looking after younger children. A boy learned fathering by watching the men and teaching younger boys. As adults, Stone Age parents could draw on the wisdom of tribal elders and a range of parenting role models.

We're not advocating a complete return to the hunter-gatherer lifestyle; even if we desired to do so, the earth is now too populated. There are, however, many lessons to be learned from the way our distant ancestors lived for about two and a half million years, as modern researchers are just now discovering. The unique techniques and guidelines in this book are based on what is now known to be essential to human happiness.

SECRETS OF OPTIMISTIC FAMILIES

Contrary to what many experts will tell you, the ideal family is not child-centered, but relationship-centered.[13] The secret to a happy, depression-proof home does not lie in focusing solely on your child at the expense of self-development and relationships with your partner and close friends, but in creating an environment that nurtures the entire family and support network. For humans young and old, relationships are everything.

A child's natural optimism is maintained in an optimistic household. If his parents see setbacks as challenges rather than defeats, believe that people can change for the better, and eschew blame, he is likely to grow up to be upbeat and optimistic.

Together, a number of key factors ensure an environment that fosters optimism in your child:

1. Parents who have a good relationship

2. Enough time with, and attention of, parents

3. Parenting styles involving empathy and consistency

4. Shared family values

5. Access to a challenging natural environment.

Good Parental Relationship

Family support, stability, and harmony will serve as a buffer against today's dysfunctional society and are the keys to your well-being and your child's resilience and future happiness. If his "tribe" is secure, he feels safe and confident; if there is friction, he fears the breakup of his family and abandonment.

Studies show that mothers are warmer and more sensitive with their babies, and fathers hold more positive attitudes toward their infants and their own roles as parents when they are in close, confiding marriages.[14] It's difficult, if not impossible, for a mother to form a solid bond with her infant if she feels unsupported or experiences friction with her partner or other important adults. Later, these relationships will serve as the template for your child's future relationships and determine whether he feels secure and able to love or anxious and socially avoidant.[15]

Time and Attention

The greatest gift you can give your child is you—your time. The very young child needs to be able to count on his primary caregivers to be consistently available and attentive so that he can form a secure attachment, first (optimally) to his mother and later his father.[16] A solid attachment is one of the strongest predictors of emotional health in the child and subsequent adult. As he grows and explores his autonomy, he needs his caregivers to be reassuringly present and available for help and encouragement in the all-consuming task of mastering his environment.

Our modern tendency to define ourselves by the number of hours we work and the dollars we earn would be puzzling to our hunter-gatherer ancestors who worked (obtained food and shelter) for only about eight to ten hours *a week*. Within the band there was always a lap for the infant or a strong arm to assist the young child.

Empathy

There's much confusion about finding the right "parenting style," for example, between being too permissive or too authoritarian. Using empathy and consistency in the ways we suggest will enable you to be warmly responsive while maintaining boundaries and appropriate control, all of which are essential to your child's optimism.

Empathy is not the same as sympathy or feeling sorry for someone. Empathy is the ability to see the world through another person's eyes and imagine what they might feel. Using empathy with your child involves understanding what he's going through, responding appropriately to his needs, and skillfully encouraging him with praise. A team led by Dr. Vicky Flory of the Australian Catholic University in Sydney showed that when parents of severely depressed and anxious children between six and thirteen were taught to improve empathy and emotional care, their children's mood disorders were considerably reduced.[17]

Parents caught up in a maelstrom of uncontrollable negative feelings may find it hard to be sensitive to others' emotional states. Yet your empathy is crucial to your child's self-awareness, self-esteem, and overall psychological adjustment.

Lack of parental empathy forces the child to compensate in dysfunctional ways. For example, if a child's crying causes his parent to be too anxious to focus on the youngster's distress, he may learn to cover up all negative feelings and thus in later life lack the skill to recognize and manage them. He may grow up unaware of his own emotions but hypersensitive to disapproval and other negative reactions in others. He may spend the rest of his life seeking understanding and acknowledgment in dysfunctional ways that make him seem demanding and self-centered, provoke discord and rejection, and reinforce his feeling of not being understood.

You can start showing—and teaching—empathy very simply when your child is an infant by "mirroring," or mimicking, him, perhaps by giving a big smile when he smiles and widening your eyes and mouth when he shows surprise. Later on, you may show empathy by encouraging him to put his feelings into words and by commiserating. Using empathy will allow you to momentarily put aside your own thoughts and feelings—your own depression, even—in order to recognize and communicate understanding of what he feels and needs.

Consistency

A child needs to be able to rely on his parents to behave predictably toward each other and him. A two-year-old will break rules to make sure that they are still being enforced. A child learns self-control through others in the family maintaining firm boundaries and being in control and reliable in their behavior.

According to noted UCLA psychiatrist and author Dr. Daniel J. Siegel, children of parents who don't show consistency may suffer from malformation in their brains in the areas dealing with emotion, memory, and relationship forming, leading to depression and serious behavioral problems.[18]

Consistency is itself a form of communication to very young children who can't yet speak and can only understand what you want through your reactions. If you don't react the same way each time, your young child will become confused and will probably get into the habit of trying to second-guess you—and other people later in life. Because second-guessing rarely works, your child will inevitably disappoint you, perhaps provoking frustration or even anger. If rules aren't consistently applied, your child won't follow them.

Almost above all, a child seeks stability, predictability, and routine. He may appreciate variety, but only within a consistent framework of relationship patterns, which are his bedrock. This desire for stasis shows up in small ways—he wants you to play the same games, read the same stories (often the same parts, in the same tone of voice), and use the same good-night ritual. You and your partner also need to be consistent in the way you relate to each other, or your child will fear that something is wrong and become anxious. When he's three or four, he may try to intervene to re-create what he perceived as the earlier, more stable, relationship between you. For example, if there is conflict between you and your partner, he may act up to divert attention from your anger.

Shared Values

Shared belief systems "are at the core of all family functioning and are powerful forces in resilience," notes University of Chicago professor Froma Walsh in her book, *Strengthening Family Resilience.*[19] Shared values, goals, rituals, and spiritual beliefs powerfully bond the family, just as they did for the hunter-gatherer tribe, and help the child feel a sense of security, belonging, and safety. Certain values have intrinsic benefits in ameliorating the negative messages of our society, which foster depression through promoting instant gratification, addictive consumerism, cynicism, and disempowerment.

A Natural Environment

Children who grow up with some contact with the natural environment tend to have fewer psychological problems—and a longer attention span—than those who do not. "Life's stressful events appear not to cause as much psychological distress in children who live in high-nature conditions compared with children who live in low-nature conditions," says Nancy Wells, assistant professor at the New York State College of Human Ecology at Cornell. "And the protective impact of nearby nature is strongest for the most vulnerable children—those experiencing the highest levels of stressful life events.

"Our data also suggest little ceiling effect with respect to the benefits of exposure to the nature environment. Even in a rural setting with a relative abundance of green landscape, more appears to be better when it comes to bolstering children's resilience against stress or adversity."[20]

As we increasingly control and plunder the planet rather than live in harmony with it, we are changing the very context that is meant to heal, teach, and shape us and our children. There are far fewer safe places today to let children romp freely, explore, and just be kids. We seem to expect children to change themselves to adapt to our increasingly frenzied and barren lifestyle rather than making sure that our society supports positive childhood experiences.

In many ways, in fact, natural childhood happiness seeking has come to be regarded as a psychiatric abnormality. Wanting to play boisterously, have adventures in nature, or make a joyful or shrieking noise is sometimes seen as attention deficit disorder (ADD/ADHD). Normal, if annoying, rambunctious behavior aimed at demanding attention and testing boundaries may be classed as conduct disorder. It's as if we need our kids to be passive, depressed, and compliant observers while we adults get on with the business of ruining our health and ecology through our out-of-control work ethic and all-pervasive consumerism.

However, enjoying any regular time in nature and getting plenty of exercise can enormously help children (and you) find a healthy equilibrium and continue to ward off depression and related mood disorders.

2

THE NEURAL CIRCUITRY OF HAPPINESS

◉

I n a very literal sense, your child's brain is programmed for future optimism or depression by her interactions with a few significant adults and older siblings.

A baby begins to be neurobiologically programmed in the womb, where the mother and baby's neurochemistry commingle, and her well-being affects her newborn's mood. Once the child is born, this intense connection continues through the attachment process.

THE ATTACHMENT DIALOGUE

When attachment is secure, a mother (or primary caregiver) is, in effect, an auxiliary brain to the infant, which develops according to the mother's emotions and responses in a dialogue that Allan Schore, a neural-psychologist and professor at the UCLA School of Medicine, calls "caregiver-infant attunement."[1] Schore describes the infant brain as "designed to be molded by the environment it encounters,"[2] which is, to a large extent, the mother.

Through this vital connection, the infant learns the how-to of the most basic and important of all human activities, forming supportive relationships: the importance of eye contact and touch and the connection between nurture (food) and love. The mother learns how to empathically tune into her child's needs.

Once the initial attachment occurs, the mother begins "downloading emotion programs into the infant's right brain. The child is using the output of the mother's right hemisphere as a template for the imprinting, the hard wiring of circuits in his own right hemisphere that will come to mediate his expanding affective [mood] capacities, an essential element of his emerging personality."[3]

This mutual shaping benefits the mother as well, for she receives a neurochemical boost that can literally make her high (through endorphins, which are part of the opioid system) and "addicted" to her baby.

Usually the primary attachment figure is the mother,[4] although a grandparent or other family member, a full-time nanny, and, of course, an adoptive parent can play this role during the first year or so of life.[5] The attachment figure need not even be female; studies show that fathers can learn to be just as responsive to young children.[6] Above all else, the child needs a sense of permanence, a sense that the people in her life will be there for her.

Whether or not the father is the main attachment figure, as the child grows, he will play a distinct and pivotal role in her physical, cognitive, and social development and provide a safe stepping-stone to the outside world in her journey to healthy autonomy.

CHILDHOOD PROGRAMMING

While the attachment process is perhaps the most potent initial factor in your child's development, she is shaped by her relationship environment in three additional ways: idealization, specialization, and whether her needs are functionally met.

Idealization

The child's instincts tell her that safety comes from being in a secure band. She will instinctually idealize you and the other significant adult members of her "tribe" (including older siblings) and seek to emulate them. Children naturally learn by imitating their elders.[7] It gives her pleasure to do what you do or to play games that in some way resemble your activities. Through the examples of adults, she learns such vital lessons as how to relate to others and which emotions and what level of self-esteem are appropriate and permissible.

Your child will also draw lessons from carefully observing your relationship with her, your partner, other involved adults, and siblings. If the parental connection is close and loving, then she will strive for caring relationships later. If the significant adults deal with their frustrations and anxieties through fighting, blaming, criticizing, excessive consumerism, drugs, or gambling, she will idealize and reproduce these behaviors—or form relationships with those who do. In all these ways, the family, or band, is the mechanism and context for learning about life and developing optimism and pessimism. She will unconsciously try to re-create these "idealized" conditions, whether they are in fact good for her or not.

Specialization

Your child's brain will also become "specialized" in dealing with certain situations and the mechanisms she develops to cope with them. These strategies, or coping mechanisms, become hard-wired in her brain through constant use and will influence her behavior throughout life.

She will re-create or seek out situations that draw on these specialized skills—even if they are totally dysfunctional. This is, for example, one reason why abused women are drawn to abusive relationships.

Needs

Another vital factor in your child's programming is whether her relationship needs are met. Although the specifics of her needs will vary according to the child's personality, circumstances, and age, they fall under four basic categories: physical safety, emotional security, attention, and importance. Feeling loved—and the ability to develop fully supportive relationships—requires that you and other adults meet her essential needs in functional and appropriate ways. If not, she may strive to get these needs met through dysfunctional coping strategies, including control, manipulation, and even illness.

AGES AND STAGES: FROM ZERO TO SIX

Some parents compete to see whose child can talk or walk first, but this is not a good idea. The truth is that all kids develop these abilities at slightly different times, and the rate at which they do so has generally nothing to do with their intelligence. The development of motor functions is intricately linked to stages of overall mastery and learning, and rushing them may impede the natural progress of other abilities. Pushing your child to be "where she ought to be" is a stressor that can trigger her into a lifelong sense of failure, pessimism, and even depression.

You can't teach a child to crawl or walk; the capacity for these skills is wired in and they occur in their own good time. What you can do, however, is provide supervised opportunities for her to explore and interact with a stimulating environment. Natural objects such as rocks and tree stumps provide excellent challenges that stimulate her to work out solutions, including using them to get upright.

Understanding your child's developmental stages before age six is very important in both creating a secure attachment and encouraging her to learn good relationships, mastery, and healthy independence—all keystones to appropriate optimism. The following overview of childhood development stages provides a very rough guide to help you build empathy with your child and provide age-appropriate opportunities for her to develop.

Birth to Three Months

Your newborn's greatest job is to be attentive, focus her senses, and bond with you or her primary caregiver. During these early months, she'll look into your eyes (a precursor of eye contact as a foundation of relationships), be absorbed by your voice and expressions, and try to imitate you. Schore says: "The child's intense interest in her face, especially in [mother's] eyes, leads him to track it in space, and to engage in periods of intense mutual gaze. The infant's gaze, in turn, reliably evokes the mother's gaze, thereby acting as a potent interpersonal channel for the transmission of reciprocal mutual influences."[8] By two or three months, she'll probably smile and respond to your joy in her—if you're her mother or primary caregiver you'll both be falling in love.

In their classic parenting manual *The Baby Book*, Dr. William and Martha Sears advocate specific techniques for strengthening this bond, including breast-feeding (which has the double benefit of reducing postnatal depression[9]), baby-wearing (carrying an infant in a pouch or sling, preferably facing you so you can make regular eye contact), and bedding with your baby.[10] At this stage, don't hesitate to pick up your infant when she cries. Her future emotional health depends on your constant support and knowing you're there. In fact, she doesn't believe that you exist if she can't see you. Dr. Sears advises that you be discerning about advice such as "Don't pick her up so much, you're spoiling her." According to Sears, much rigid and extreme baby training is to "help baby become more 'convenient.' It is based on the misguided assumption that babies cry to manipulate, not to communicate."[11]

Crying is your baby's language, and soon your empathy will enable you to distinguish between cries of pain, hunger, and fear, which will help you become a more confident parent. She'll turn her head when she hears your voice and react to noise, motion, and light. Expose her to a wide range of stimuli such as soft toys, gentle music, and the outdoors so she becomes more aware of her surroundings.

Stimulated by your responses, your baby's brain is doubling its size in the first year, constantly forming new cells and making millions of new connections between them as she takes in information from her experience and learns about this strange place she's arrived at.

In early infancy, because her father sees and treats the baby as an individual, not an extension of her mother, this relationship helps the baby begin to develop a sense of self and other, which in coming months prepares her for a life apart from mother.[12]

Three to Six Months

At this age, your baby will stare wide-eyed at everything and anyone who is looking at her. She is trying to make sense of her world on the basis of her previous—and obviously limited—experiences. She'll recognize you and giggle if you make a funny face. She may begin to take interest in things outside of herself, showing a preference for a particular toy or object. She can amuse herself for short periods of time in her crib, swing, or infant seat and is beginning to realize she can do things for herself.

She will begin to notice the emotions of other people and will react to your tone of voice, becoming upset with an angry voice and pleased with a happy tone.

On a cognitive level, your baby will begin to realize that you exist even if she can't see you (psychologists call this "object permanence"). You can help her with this understanding by playing peek-a-boo. She's starting to learn cause and effect and, most important, that she can influence her world. For example, she'll drop toys and search for them and make a noise with everything that she can—always looking to you for approval.

Babies of both sexes will become excited by active and up-tempo play with Dad, though boys tend to be more willing than girls to play a scary game such as making monster faces. During these games, an infant starts to learn to manage intense feelings and shift emotional gears, helping her develop a sense of competence and mastery.[13] Dad's positive involvement during this period leads to more secure attachment later on.[14]

Now is also the time she may start to show anxiety when strangers are around. She will begin to notice that people are different—before, they've all been the same. She may get frightened when she is picked up by anyone other than Mom, Dad, and her regular caregivers, even if they've often done so.

She'll also appreciate being read to, even if she can't understand a word. She'll respond to photographs and pictures with bold, bright colors. She wants to turn pages as you read. Since music and language are closely related, she'll love the rhythm of nursery rhymes.

Six to Nine Months

Your baby will probably begin to crawl, her weight gain will slow, and she may seem more interested in toying with food than eating it. As she refines her motor skills, using her thumb (probably for the first time), she needs plenty of interesting things to play with. No longer passive, she'll start to display a range of complex emotions, such as annoyance and anger if you take away a favorite toy. When she sees you, she'll coo and gurgle excitedly and reach out to be picked up.

She wants to be picked up by Dad[15] and enjoys the adventurous, physically stimulating, and unpredictable play with him that leads to rapid cognitive development. His use of shorter, more rapid staccato bursts of verbal communication will also stimulate her brain to grow and learn and improve her thinking skills.[16] In fact, perhaps because Dad is not quite so attuned to an infant's needs as Mom, the baby will work more actively to make her needs known, learning valuable lessons in communication and relationships.

At this stage, she'll also begin to take an active interest in other people and the world around her and may try to mimic tones and inflections she hears in other people's voices. Introduce her to new places and people, but remember that she still may become anxious and need your reassurance when being touched or picked up by strangers. As she begins to interact more with her environment, your child needs you to constantly demonstrate that your relationship with her is still OK. Return her smile, take her outstretched hand, join in her games.

Nine to Twelve Months

This is the beginning of the active exploration stage, and your little one is probably constantly on the move. She is driven by curiosity and a fear that brings her toddling back to mother. Child-proof the area and let her get on with it. She'll never range more than one hundred feet away from you and will prefer to stay within sight. She's probably busy practicing all the complex elements of standing up—don't rush her, allow her to stumble and make mistakes, and avoid baby walkers. Give her lots of things to lever herself up on.

Self-esteem will begin to emerge. She'll probably be fixated on her image, kissing or patting her reflection in the mirror. She needs lots of positive encouragement from you—clap your hands when she does something new and praise her lavishly. She wants you to participate in things now, not just stand by and watch her.

Laying down firm, consistent limits takes on new importance. She'll begin testing boundaries—a process that will continue through the twos and threes—and you may find this annoying. However, don't be too strict; save the hard-and-fast rules for later. Stay attuned to her preferences, and, except where safety or your own needs are concerned, let her have her way. She's growing more independent, but also more demanding. It's important to encourage independence and exploration while at the same time making sure she knows you're there for her. At this stage, if her primary relationship is with Mom, she'll prefer her father over strangers, though she is not as likely to fret when Dad is absent as she is if Mom is away.[17]

She'll also probably be able to understand more and more words and link them to gestures and objects. This is the time of "bye, bye," "Mama," "Dada," and, frustratingly, "no!" She'll probably be increasingly annoyed when she doesn't get her way, and the first tantrums may appear.

Twelve to Eighteen Months

Now that she can walk, she'll be a bit more of a handful. She'll increasingly test boundaries, and you need to be really firm, yet gentle and consistent, swiftly letting her know what you need. She has little long-term memory yet, so don't try to discipline her for anything that she did wrong more than a few minutes ago. The tantrums will be more frequent. She's beginning to realize that there are things she's not allowed to do and will readily show her displeasure when thwarted. Above all now, she'll need consistency—bath at the same time, bed at the same time, meals at the same time. Let her see you cooking or running the bath to reinforce this routine.

Her mental ability will be developing fast; she knows many objects by name and what they're used for. You can help this process along by joining in; for example, point to objects and say their names.

Somewhere between fourteen and seventeen months, a profound shift takes place in the mother-father-child dynamic. This period marks the beginning of the first stage of separation from mother. Both boys and girls become aware of their father as a male, and in their different ways each sets out to forge a relationship with him. A boy's need to identify with his father intensifies, and he will often turn to Dad rather than Mom in times of stress for what child psychiatrist Dr. James Herzog calls "emotional refueling." A girl, too, will turn to her father at this age, "increasing her efforts to show him how to relate to her."[18] Entry to toddlerhood will require mother's conscious acceptance and readiness to share her child with the father; trust in the value of his involvement; and control over her own natural jealousy, as the child establishes a bond with Dad and other significant adults.

Eighteen Months to Two Years

Get ready for the "terrible twos": your adorable cherub may soon metamorphose into a terror. She may already be misbehaving, especially if she's afraid or upset or if her routine has been interrupted. She realizes that through her behaviors she can affect your mood, of which she is a very accurate judge. She'll need quality time with you—sitting beside you when you read a book together, for example. This is not the time to take away the favorite toy or blanket that may go wherever she does.

She's now ready to recognize emotions and needs help with identifying and expressing them. Learning to accept and show feelings is vital to emotional health, and suppressing them often leads to depression. Talk appropriately about your own emotions ("Mommy is very happy") and even those of her toys ("Teddy is sad because it's raining and he can't go out and play!"). As part of her awareness of self and others, she'll observe father's appreciation of mother as distinct from his relationship with her. She may also begin to understand the idea of something happening now and something happening later.

Her sense of self-esteem and individuation is apparent through her new favorite word: "no!" She's learning that she has control over herself and her environment and that she's an individual. However, you are still the ideal, so she'll follow you around the house doing what you do. Encourage her to join in.

Two Years

Expect everything above but more so. Tantrums and potty training also mark this stage (don't rush her).

Her growing autonomy will result in defiance (which will lessen when she goes to preschool and completes the first stage of separation). Suppress your instinct to overprotect or interfere too much, and allow the gradual process of letting go of your child. Your toddler may fuss at length over what she wears, plays with, or eats, and bedtime and bath times may become trials of will. She wants to be boss. Although she recognizes other people and will play creatively and engage with kids her age, it's still too early for her to make friends. You and other caregivers now need to decide the areas in which it's OK for her to make choices—over what she wears, for example, or what she eats for breakfast. The ability to make informed choices begins at this age and should be encouraged. Her vocabulary now probably exceeds four hundred words, and she can begin to form sentences. She may understand what you're saying to her but pretend not to. Remember to phrase everything in simple, concrete terms.

Three

At this age, she discovers friends, and play dates will become an important part of her routine and socialization. She should gradually become more caring and sensitive to others' feelings—even yours! Teaching empathy could involve asking, "How do you think your friend feels when you call her a crybaby?" Or saying "Daddy is really happy when you give him a kiss." Imaginary friends may appear, often taking the blame for things that your angel has done wrong, but also comforting and helping her come to terms with reality. Allow her imagination full rein; take an interest in her "friend."

This is also the time of the second most annoying word in childhood's lexicon: "why?" Often the questions are more about testing the relationship with you than curiosity. She'll want you to dialogue with her and take her into the decision-making process. She should now become a part of the Family Powwow (see Chapter 7), and she'll learn a more balanced view of the world by observing each parent's different approaches to problem-solving and tasks.

Four

As the process of separation truly begins, your child will flip-flop between wanting to be independent and back in the safety of your arms. Don't rush preschool or force parties with unfamiliar kids. She's no longer a baby and will react badly to being told that she's acting like one. Take time to prepare her for being apart from you, and discuss her fears. Use your empathy. Never tell her that her feelings are wrong.

She will begin to understand more complicated instructions such as "put the lid on the box" (which includes three concepts—a lid, a box, and an action), and her vocabulary will extend to more than fifteen hundred words (some of them ones you'd rather she didn't know!). Reading to her becomes even more important. Talk to her at mealtimes; don't ignore her presence or get angry when this chatterbox wants to join in. Take the time to really listen to her.

By the age of four and five, both boys and girls will crave more acknowledgment from their father—who is often the only available male role model—as a way of further defining their masculinity and femininity. A girl may become resentful or jealous of her mother and even act in a flirtatious way with Dad. Both of you may find this difficult to cope with, but his appropriate responses and attention will set her up for the kind of romantic or sexual relationships she will have in her teens and beyond. Be clear about your boundaries with both male and female children, as this is how they get their safety.

Five and Six

"I want to pick my own friends!" This is the age of increased socializing and seeking out friends independently. It's also a time for increasingly cooperative games, where roles are assigned and group decisions are made. To a large extent, you can step back and allow this to happen, just encouraging her if she's shy.

By six, she will have mastered around twenty-five hundred words and can understand quite complicated sentences, though generalizations and concepts may still be confusing.

At this time, her brain is about 80 percent fully formed, and her personality is more or less fixed (though it can change in response to repeated or traumatic outside stimuli). She will soon become an apprentice adult and is keen to learn grown-up things. Her increasing ability to deal with separation allows her now to go to school without psychological harm.

Your role is to protect her from the most harmful outside influences and encourage her to become a full member of your band by bringing her more and more into the decision-making process. Give her simple tasks and chores so that she continues to feel she's an important member of the household. You need to make sure she knows how to say "no" to people outside as well as inside the family and to maintain proper boundaries—which you largely do by maintaining your own limits in your relationship with her. She is still learning by example.

Your child will go on to learn new things and grow in exciting ways. However, as we will see, the basics of her personality and capacity for resilience and optimism are by now largely in place.

3

THE REAL CAUSES OF CHILDHOOD (AND LATER) DEPRESSION

◉

U ntil recently, there were no studies on depression in young children— in fact, as recently as the early 1990s, the majority of health professionals assumed that toddlers didn't suffer from depression, because their symptoms weren't as obvious as those of older children and adults.

However, depression in young children is now a burgeoning area of academic inquiry—and controversy. In fact, the very definition of depression at any age is attracting heated debate as more and more conditions fall under its umbrella, including chronic anxiety, a wide range of physical symptoms,[1] and perhaps even posttraumatic stress disorder (PTSD).[2] Researchers estimate that 80 percent of all people who see doctors suffer from "somatized" depression—physical symptoms that have no physiological basis.[3]

In the midst of today's depression epidemic, it's no wonder that, through no fault of our own, our children are being affected by mood disorders.

DEPRESSION IN THE WOMB

According to Canadian reproductive psychiatry expert Shaila Misri, M.D., and others, depression can begin in the womb.[4] Stress hormones find their way from the mother to the fetus, causing the child to be born depressed or anxious or with a disposition to become so. When a girl grows up, she may also pass on her stress hormones to the next generation, creating behavioral problems, anxiety, and depression in her children.[5] However, studies show that if a mother of a depressed infant heals from depression, so probably will her child.[6]

If you are free from significant strain, happy to be pregnant, and surrounded by people who express their love and excitement about the upcoming event, you will send the fetus positive and health-giving neurochemical messages.

The mother's alcohol and drug problems may cause her babies to be addicted at birth or later in life.[7] If a mother is using SSRIs (powerful antidepressants known as selective serotonin reuptake inhibitors) to control her mood, her child can suffer withdrawal symptoms and other effects at birth.[8]

Again, it's the context. The context of a fetus is the womb, and he is going to be affected by his mother's stress and coping behaviors, use of drugs, state of relationships, work satisfaction, health, and mood. As we've seen, these factors affect and shape the child long after birth. However, our seven-step program can help you ensure a happy, depression-free child.

IS YOUR CHILD DEPRESSED?

Spotting your child's depression may not be easy, and even your pediatrician may miss it. According to a study reported in the *Journal of Pediatric Health Care*, 83 percent of pediatricians fail to pick up on the illness.[9] Every child is different, and children react differently at different ages—or even on different days! Your child's depression might show up as sadness and listlessness or as irritability and defiance—or even as a consistent stomachache or headache that your doctor can't explain.

Depression can also show up as sleeplessness and anxiety or regressive behaviors such as bed-wetting at the age of six. More than 70 percent of children diagnosed with ADHD are also depressed or anxious,[10] and some experts, including ourselves, believe that many behaviors classed as ADHD are just how depression shows up in boys. Certainly, both are frequently misdiagnosed.[11]

Catching the symptoms of early depression may be difficult, but it's vital to your child's well-being, not only now but later. Experts agree that early depression is a strong predictor of later depression and that the earlier you notice this illness the easier it is to overcome.

The following list of possible depression symptoms may be helpful in discovering your child's depression now or risk factors for later problems. Always check with your pediatrician to make sure your child is not suffering a physical disease, since illness often causes temporary depressive symptoms. Bear in mind that not all the symptoms are relevant to all ages and that this list works better for ages three and older.

The core features of depression in very young children appear in a similar, but age-adjusted fashion to how they appear in adults. For example, children have more fluctuating mood states than adults during the course of any given day,[12] and you won't discern guilt or hopelessness in infants or difficulty in decision-making in the first few years.

Signs of Depression in Young Children
Feelings: Does he express or exhibit

- Less pleasure than he used to from activities and play or no pleasure (anhedonia)

- Sadness

- Low energy and/or recent changes in energy level

- Worthlessness or low self-esteem

- Hopelessness

- Guilt

Thinking: Is he having difficulty

- Concentrating

- Making decisions

Physical Problems: Does he complain of

- Stomachaches

- Headaches

- Lack of energy

- Sleeping problems

- Weight or appetite changes

Behavioral Problems: Does he display

- Excessive crying

- Restlessness

- Grouchiness and irritability

- The desire to be alone most of the time

- Play themes involving death or suicide

- Difficulty making friends or getting along with others

DEPRESSION CAUSES

Although a child's genetic makeup may play a significant role in determining his level of depression and resilience,[13] almost all experts agree that severe stress and childhood trauma are at the root of both childhood and adult depression.[14]

Recently, scientists actually discovered a gene they believe underlies much of depression: a variant of the serotonin transporter gene 5-HTT. But having this gene probably doesn't cause depression on its own, it simply makes some children more likely to become depressed if they experience certain stresses.[15]

Nearly all researchers agree that if your child experiences sufficient difficult or traumatic events, he can become depressed with or without the genetic variant. A gene such as this one is like a switch that can be turned on, or off, by environmental factors.[16] The trick for parents is to make sure the switch isn't easily turned on.

So, what kinds of events produce harmful stress or trauma in a child and turn on the genetic switch for depression now or later? There is no precise formula for how much stress or what particular trauma will cause depression. We usually look for a pattern of events, not just single occurrences. Some stressful events may have little long-lasting effect if they are short-lived and addressed quickly and appropriately. All children are different, and even children from the same household may react differently to the same stressor. No child is born into exactly the same household, because each sibling enters the family at a different time, often with other siblings already there. According to Peter W. Nathanielsz, author of *Life in the Womb: The Origin of Health and Disease*, even twins can experience different conditioning *in utero*.[17]

DEPRESSION TRIGGERS
IN YOUNG CHILDREN

Unfortunately, our culture has so undermined and strained the modern family—while at the same time removing its traditional supports—that stressors and traumas abound. Significant stressors that can affect young children include:

- Parents' depression

- Early maternal separation, rejection, or ambivalence

- Insecure attachment

- Divorce or family conflict, including violence or threats of violence

- Death or illness in the family

- Too little time with primary caregivers

- Threat of abandonment

- Physical abuse, including physical punishment or the threat of it and overly rough treatment from siblings

- Persistent criticism

- Lack of appropriate praise and encouragement

- Inhibition to expressing feelings

- Lack of clear or consistent boundaries

- Parental addiction

- Ostracism, teasing, or bullying by family members or playmates

- Lack of opportunities for contact with nature

- Being required to sit still for long periods of time

- "Parentalization"—having to parent his parent or younger siblings

- Constant relocation

- Violent neighborhood

- Too much TV or inappropriate media

- Not having needs met functionally for safety, emotional security, attention, or importance

Even behaviors in families that might seem innocuous can be damaging and can lead to depression. A seminal 2002 American Academy of Pediatrics (AAP) report defines trauma as "a repeated pattern of damaging interactions between parent(s) [or, we assume, other siblings and significant adults] and child that becomes typical of the relationship." This includes anything that causes the child to feel not worthwhile, not loveable, or insecure (and even endangered), or as if his only value lies in meeting someone else's needs. Examples cited in the report include "belittling, degrading, or ridiculing a child; making him or her feel unsafe; failing to express affection, caring, and love; neglecting mental health, medical, or educational needs."[18] According to the AAP, childhood trauma can also include witnessing domestic, community, and televised violence. Two researchers, Robert Marvin and John Byng-Hall, indicate that negative family interactions such as secrets, internal conflicts, and parents' lack of cohesiveness as authorities in the family also affect the child's ability to form healthy attachment bonds and, thus, his ongoing emotional well-being.[19]

THREE DEGREES OF SEPARATION

One of the major bulwarks against depression throughout life is the security of the early bond with the primary caregiver. No young hunter-gatherer child would have ever been parted from his band; women took their babies wherever they went. Now, economic and career pressures or lifestyle choices are making early mother/child separation a common reality.

"Most people think that it does no harm to go away and leave a very young child, because they feel the baby does not know the difference. This is not true," said eminent child authority Dr. Lee Salk in her 1973 landmark book *What Every Child Would Like His Parents to Know*. "In fact, the opposite is true. The very young child does know, vividly. Because he has very little concept of 'now' and 'later' a baby does not understand that if you go away you will ultimately come back. If he cannot see you, you are no longer there; in fact, you don't exist."[20]

Although even a short separation may cause the young infant temporary anxiety, this will pass and doesn't mean you can't take a break. In fact, taking some time for yourself, for a shower, a brisk walk, or a brief meeting, is vital to your well-being and, thus, to your child's.

Parents today are much more aware, but many are still not clear, about how maternal separation can affect a young child's well-being and development. John Bowlby, the father of attachment theory, wrote that there are three distinct stages in separation anxiety: protest or anger, despair, and detachment.[21] More recent studies are confirming his findings.[22]

Protest is shown in a child's refusal to accept a substitute for the mother or primary caregiver, in tearful and violent crying, and in constant vigilance for their return.

While his parents went on a week's holiday, eighteen-month-old Benjamin was left with his aunt and uncle, whom he did not know well. By the second night of his stay, he had trouble sleeping, and his daytime mood was, according to his uncle, "cranky and stubborn."

Despair, phase two of separation anxiety, is marked by moaning, weeping, and sad facial expressions. The child is obviously depressed. As Benjamin's stay with his relatives wore on, he became increasingly anxious and despondent. His play became more constricted; he smiled less and less; and he spent long periods of time standing around forlornly, even though his uncle tried to engage him in a number of activities his parents had said he enjoyed. After a week, Benjamin was returned to his parents, but he remained clingy and regressive for several months.

According to Bowlby, detachment, the third phase, can begin as early as seven days after separation. The longer the period of separation, the longer this phase lasts, and the more damage it does. The young child seems to stop seeking her mother, becomes apathetic, and may even shut down all emotions. This behavior masks rage and may be a defense—which can last for hours, days, or a lifetime—against the agony of ever loving, and ever losing, again. Absence makes the heart grow frozen, not fonder.[23]

Different children not only react differently to separation, they react differently day to day. Three-and-a-half-year-old Chloe had just spent a couple of hours at nursery school before arriving at her friend's house to play. Her mother, assuming Chloe would be fine without her for an extra hour or two, had made plans to do some shopping. After an hour at her playmate's house, however, Chloe began to ask repeatedly for her mother and to refuse adult comforting. She showed her sense of loss through disruptive behaviors, such as throwing toys at her playmate. Chloe's mother was almost as dismayed as her child on her return—and surprised. She'd been gone from Chloe for the same length of time on several previous occasions.

Deciding whether or not a young child can spend time away from his primary caregiver requires sensitivity to the child's needs as well as insight and flexibility—in short, empathy. Gradually preparing the child for separation, over a length of time, helps. However, it is not true, as some self-help books suggest, that preparation allows the infant to be separated without some degree of trauma. (For advice to working mothers, see Chapters 5 and 17.)

An absent father, or one who consistently works late, also causes significant problems.[24] The child doesn't understand the logical reasons—such as his parents' desire to work hard to secure his education. He simply feels rejected and that somehow he's not worthy of his parents' love. Not only does this engender guilt (fertile ground for depression), it sets him up later to seek people who represent these ideals through their physical or emotional unavailability.

To a hunter-gatherer child in a hostile environment, abandonment meant death. This innate dread of rejection and abandonment is often at the heart of depression at any age.

TRAUMA AND THE CHILD'S BRAIN

How do acute childhood stress and trauma set the conditions for lifelong depression, anxiety, and PTSD, an extreme form of anxiety? As we've seen, early separation can lead to the death of some brain cells, but that's not the only mechanism. Stress and trauma actually inhibit proper development of vital areas of the brain.

The amygdala is a part of the limbic system and has the job of sending powerful emotional warning signals to the central cortex (the command and control center of the brain) and central nervous system, thus ensuring a response even before danger is consciously noticed. In a process that Daniel Goleman, author of *Emotional Intelligence*, calls an "amygdala hijack," the amygdala of the traumatized or depressed child becomes overactive, overwhelming the brain with continuous alarm messages.[25]

Under prolonged stress, the central cortex slows down and fails to switch off these alarm signals, even when danger has passed, leading to a prolonged period of anxiety, depression, or PTSD.

To make matters worse, in the stressed and traumatized brain, the hippocampus, another part of the limbic system, is too small. It doesn't have enough cells—neurons—to properly do its job of helping the person remember how he successfully handled previously stressful or depressing situations.

WHY ANTIDEPRESSANTS
AREN'T THE ANSWER

Perhaps because very young children are too young to benefit from the standard psychotherapeutic approaches to depression such as Interpersonal Therapy and Cognitive Behavioral Therapy, or perhaps because of the major marketing efforts of drug companies, pediatricians are increasingly prescribing SSRIs such as Prozac, Paxil (Aropax), and Zoloft for preschoolers.

However, according to a clinical review of the evidence published in 2004 in the prestigious *British Medical Journal* (*BMJ*), there is *no scientific evidence whatsoever* that SSRIs work for children of this age range (or indeed for anyone under age eighteen).[26] What's more, they may well cause great harm; most are banned for children in Great Britain.

A study by the Food and Drug Administration (FDA) came to similar conclusions as the *BMJ*. "These are sobering findings and certainly raise a question about the benefits of these drugs in pediatric depression," the FDA's Dr. Thomas Laughren wrote in a January 2004 memo.[27] The FDA has also insisted on labeling packets of antidepressants with a warning that they may lead to child suicide. Yet despite all these cautions, large quantities of antidepressants are still doled out to this age group.

Glenn McIntosh of Austin, Texas, whose daughter Caitlin, twelve, hanged herself with shoelaces weeks after being started on Paxil and then switched to Zoloft, told the *Washington Post*: "We were told that Paxil and Prozac were wonder drugs. We were lied to."[28]

Parents are particularly angry that data on the link between antidepressants and suicide had appeared in professional journals for sixteen years before the FDA took action.[29]

While pharmaceutical companies insist that antidepressants are not addictive, research has shown that the brain becomes habituated to them, and coming off antidepressants can cause severe symptoms even in adults—just as with crack cocaine.[30]

Scientists have also uncovered new risks concerning antidepressants in adults that may well apply to children. In a 2003 study led by immunology professor John Gordon of Birmingham University, SSRIs were linked to brain tumors.[31] In a 2004 study, Dr. Welmoed Meijer of the Dutch Utrecht Institute for Pharmaceutical Sciences and colleagues found "a significant association between the degree of serotonin reuptake inhibition by antidepressants and risk of hospital admission for abnormal bleeding."[32]

While antidepressants are probably not an effective solution to child depression, please don't forget that you are in no way powerless against this illness now or later. The next seven chapters explain the core of our comprehensive program to ensure your child's well-being, now and in the future.

PART II

SEVEN STEPS TO DEPRESSION-PROOF YOUR CHILD— FOR LIFE

4

STEP 1:
DON'T LET YOUR
INNER SABOTEUR
AFFECT YOUR FAMILY

◉

"Why can't you leave me alone for *two minutes*? You're becoming such a spoiled brat!" Samantha ranted at four-year-old Christie, who had run into her mother's study to show her a drawing for the fourth time in ten minutes while Samantha was on her third attempt to balance the family checkbook. Seeing Christie's frozen face and quivering lip, Samantha buried her own face in her hands.

"I thought, how could I *say* such a thing? Christie was just being a little girl wanting her Mommy," she later said in a session to Alicia. "And then I realized, my God, that's exactly what my mother used to say to me, in just that tone of voice! I swore I would never be like her, and sometimes it's as if it's her voice coming of my mouth!"

Most parents we know have had similar experiences. "One of the unspoken trials of parenthood is that it brings out elements of our psychology that seem to take over despite our best intentions, often compelling us to behave in ways with our children that replicate what we experienced with our parents" writes psychologist and author Robert Karen.[1]

These self-defeating beliefs and behaviors are part of the self-reinforcing system we call the "inner saboteur." As they say about alcohol in Alcoholics Anonymous (AA), the inner saboteur is "cunning, devious, and powerful."

At times it even seems to have a will of its own, so strong is the compulsion within us to re-create the past.

Changing negative parenting patterns requires courage, insight, determination, and persistence—but you can do it! Overcoming the inner saboteur is vital to your child's lifelong well-being and in some cases her freedom from depression. Remember that your problematic behavioral patterns *are not your fault.* As explained in Chapter 2, the young child that you were had no control over how your environment shaped your brain or the lifelong patterns that resulted.

To ensure that the burdens from your past are not placed on your children's shoulders, you must become keenly aware of your negative patterns, their origins, and the three ways your inner saboteur shows up day to day at home.

Three Ways the Inner Saboteur Can Affect Your Child

1. **Idealization:** You unwittingly apply the dysfunctional parenting styles, beliefs, and behaviors—even perhaps using the very words—of your parents or other significant adults from childhood.

2. **Transference:** You react to other people—including your child—as if they were significant figures from your own past.

3. **Coping Mechanisms:** In order to use coping mechanisms developed as a young child and adopt familiar roles, you subconsciously re-create within your present family the circumstances of your family of origin.

UNDERSTANDING IDEALIZATION

You are genetically wired to idealize and adopt the parenting styles, beliefs, and behaviors—even the language—of your own early caregivers. If your parents believed "children should be seen and not heard," it will probably be a struggle for you to encourage your kids to chime in at the dinner table, especially if, like most healthy kids, they are boisterous and compete for your attention. If your parents were more laissez-faire, you may hesitate to put firm, consistent boundaries in place.

Many aspects of your hand-me-down parenting program may be quite useful, particularly if your parents were empathic, skilled, and relatively happy. And you've probably worked hard not to replicate some of the things your parents did that have caused you pain. Still, the inner saboteur may trick you into repeating some of their less positive responses.

When her much-loved daughter came to her for attention, Samantha in a moment of stress saw Christie as her own mother had described herself as a child . . . a "spoiled brat." The criticism left Samantha's mouth before her consciousness could recognize what was going on and stop it. Score: Inner Saboteur one; Samantha nil. However, Samantha realized quickly what had happened and comforted Christie and then shared the problem and discussed strategies for preventing it from happening again with another appropriate person, Alicia. Score three for Samantha.

Take a moment to remember, and perhaps write down, the following ways your own past may be influencing your family:

- What are some positive things about your parents' parenting style?

- What are some of the negative things?

- Which of these are part of your own parenting style?

AVOIDING TRANSFERENCE

Transference is a well-known psychological term referring to the patient's inevitable projection of childhood figures onto the therapist. But transference isn't limited to the therapist's office; you can project characteristics of people from your past onto everyone, including your child.

Projection occurs because the brain doesn't have a generalized capacity for making relationships but forms early on a few specific templates into which it later tries to fit all relationships. A child raised in a tightly knit hunter-gatherer band might form up to forty such templates, whereas a child brought up in a two- or even one-parent nuclear family might have only a very few role models, depending on the number of significant adults, including older siblings, around.

As a result, your unconscious seeks out people who seem similar to early idealized figures or tries to fit current relationships into those roles.[2] You may, therefore, react to your partner—or your boss or your child's kindergarten teacher—as if she were your stern, authoritarian father. You may respond to your child as if she were either yourself as a child or perhaps your own very demanding mother.

"In every nursery there are ghosts," writes Selma Fraiberg, a prominent child psychoanalyst and author of *The Magic Years*, such that "a parent and his child may find themselves re-enacting a moment or a scene from another time with another set of characters."[3]

The process can begin even before birth. Arietta Slade, an attachment theorist looking at mothers' fantasies about their unborn children, reported that "a mother who felt controlled by her mother her entire life is already preoccupied with whether she can control her fetus. Or a mother whose own mother pushed her aside is already convinced that her child won't have any needs, won't change her life, and will be autonomous early on. Chills go up and down your spine when you hear these things."[4]

Transference plays havoc with relationships between parents. "I'd come home from a hard day at work and start to tell my wife about a new account I'd won, and every two sentences were interrupted by the baby wanting attention," Carl told Bob during a session. "Valerie would get this dreamy look on her face and it's as if I wasn't there. For an instant I wanted to storm out of the house, slam the door, and not come back. I actually caught myself thinking, 'No one ever looked at me like that!' as if I were a little kid. Then I remembered that's exactly how I felt when Mom brought my baby sister home when I was five. But I still couldn't help feeling guilty and ashamed, and later that night I was cold and distancing to Valerie, as if she were my mother who I'd felt had betrayed me!"

The process of understanding how transference affects your parenting involves asking yourself:

- What characteristics—good and bad—does your partner share with a significant childhood figure? Do you respond to your partner in some of the same ways? Could that account for the strength and irrationality of some of your responses?

- Does your child evoke similar feelings as someone from your past? Or do you find yourself acting with your child as your parents did with you?

- How do other people in your life (mother-in-law, boss, nanny, and so on) remind you of significant figures?

Tip: When you get into an argument with your partner or start yelling at your child, stop and ask yourself: "Who in the past am I really fighting with? Who in the past am I yelling at?"

DISCOVERING DYSFUNCTIONAL COPING MECHANISMS

Faced with problematic situations and relationships, a child develops behavioral coping mechanisms in order to try to get her needs met. The more difficult the relationship, the more effort the child has to make, and the more neurons (brain cells) become involved. As a result, she literally becomes specialized in these kinds of relationships. To apply her specialized skills, and because the familiar seems safe (even when it's not), as an adult she will often seek to re-create within her own family the most difficult relationships and circumstances of childhood. For example, a child who was forced to adopt the role of peacekeeper between arguing parents may later do anything to make her child and partner happy, even at her own expense. (She may even adopt a peacekeeping role at work or avoid conflict to her own detriment.) Her child may go on to do the same thing with her family. Thus, we pass our programs on to our children and our children's children, creating a "linear tribe" down through generations.

To begin to discover your own childhood coping mechanisms that are now adult patterns, ask yourself:

- Which significant adult(s) did you have to try hard to please as a child, perhaps because he or she was emotionally or physically unavailable?

- What role did you take, or what coping mechanism did you adopt, in relation to this person to try to get your needs met?

- What coping mechanism or role from the past do you adopt today, and with whom, even if it no longer works for you?

RE-CREATING THE PAST

The first signs of discord between Mick and Jacinta occurred after the birth of Angelica and, one year later, Emily. The added strains of a larger family caused Jacinta to feel out of control and insist on an obsessive level of tidiness that seemed to grow in proportion to its unfeasibility in a household with a three- and four-year-old. She was increasingly critical of Mick and the kids and would burst into tears, complaining it was "all too much. I can't handle it!" Mick, who tended to deal with emotions by not having any, withdrew from a growing sense of helplessness and guilt by spending more time at work.

The couple's habitual patterns—their inner saboteurs—prevented them from fully supporting each other or meeting their daughters' needs for affection, attention, and empathy. Each child developed her own coping mechanisms. Angelica defended herself against the pain of emotional abandonment and not being able to please her mother by simply no longer trying. She seemed nonchalant around her mother, asked for little, spent most of her time on her own, and seemed uninterested in her playmates at nursery school. Noting her withdrawn behavior, her pediatrician suggested she might be depressed. Little Emily took the opposite tack, becoming demanding, obstinate, and clingy and resorting to tantrums when she didn't get her own way.

Working with Bob, the couple discovered the childhood roots of their patterns and how these were currently being triggered. Jacinta's mother had five children close together in age, valued tidiness above all else, and often flew into rages at the inevitable chaos. Jacinta's obsessiveness resulted partly from following this ideal and partly from trying to create some sense of control in her out-of-control environment. Jacinta's father was away much of the time on work-related travel, and her parents divorced when she was six, leaving her with a lifelong fear of abandonment.

Unfortunately, Mick's tendency to withdraw emotionally and work long hours reinforced Jacinta's unconscious association between him and her father. Mick's father avoided open confrontation with his critical mother by simply leaving the room or house whenever disagreement threatened—a pattern Mick idealized and tried to emulate.

The astute reader will also note that the two girls were already mirroring their parents, with Angelica becoming withdrawn like her father and Emily angry and prone to outbursts like her mother.

DEFEATING THE INNER SABOTEUR

Once you externalize the problem, that is, once you realize that *neither these feelings nor behaviors are really yours*, but come from early circumstances over which you had no control, it's often easier to confront them and think creatively about how to prevent them from being triggered. You can then look realistically at a situation and ask: How is my filter from childhood distorting how I see these people and my options, and is this really true? Jacinta asked herself, "Is my life really out of control if my kids behave like kids and make a mess?" After talking to Bob, her answer was "Of course not! The real disruption came from long ago and had nothing to do with them."

Once the couple realized that the intensity of their feelings and some of their behavior were holdovers from the past, they were able to step back and work out strategies for managing both. Jacinta became more relaxed about normal household disruptions and untidiness. She let Mick know exactly what he needed to do in order to reassure the small child within that he would not abandon her, which included calling twice a day from work to say he loved her, holding her when she got upset rather than leaving, and not bringing work home on the weekends. She agreed to keep her tone of voice level even when irritated or upset, so as not to trigger his fear of conflict. Both agreed to tell each other what they were feeling before emotions and actions escalated.

As the parental relationship improved and they became emotionally stronger and more flexible, Jacinta and Mick were able to be more tolerant and empathetic with both children and to better meet their needs. They made strong efforts to catch themselves whenever their inner saboteurs threatened to impact the kids, took time daily to discuss parenting strategies and concerns, and spent much more time on family activities as well as one on one with the girls. With a lot of encouragement from Mom and special activities with Dad, Angelica emerged from her shell and began talking about her feelings, participating in family activities, and making new friends at school. Emily learned to ask clearly and calmly for what she wanted and became much less easily frustrated when denied.

"We may not be the perfect family," Mick later reported to Bob. "But the kids know we're there for them, and we talk things through. By catching these problems now, I believe we've dramatically changed the course of all our lives for the better."

Over the course of the next six chapters, you will learn many more techniques for stopping the inner saboteur from affecting your family, including how to make sure your relationships support you and your child instead of re-creating past patterns. But for now take these actions:

1. Make a list of ways you relate to members of your present family that you feel could be improved.

2. Ask your partner to do the same.

3. Discuss these lists.

4. Decide how you'll help each other resolve the issues underlying these actions and go against these patterns.

5. Stay vigilant and discuss your progress, praising each other when you see improvements.

STEP 2: DETERMINE A HEALTHY BALANCE BETWEEN WORK AND FAMILY

◉

Nowhere does the mismatch between our Stone Age genes and our jet age lifestyle show up more painfully than in the modern struggle to marry two often seemingly incompatible aspects of our lives—work and family.

Our hunter-gatherer ancestors experienced no divide between the work they did to provide food and shelter (which usually took no more than twelve hours a week), caring for their children, socializing, and engaging in rituals. Babies were carried while the women gathered and gossiped, and when the mother needed a break, grandmothers and companions were delighted to take a turn. To her female ancestors, the plight of today's frantic mother, who must choose isolation and lack of status at home as a full-time mom or tear herself away from her children and juggle their needs against that of her own career, would probably evoke horror and pity. And these are the lucky mothers whose financial circumstances or other supports allow them the choice!

Allocating time to work, home, and self-care is perhaps the most vital ongoing decision you and your partner will make regarding your children's well-being and resistance to depression. For example, do you organize parenthood around work or work around parenthood? Making the best choice requires correct information, self-awareness, some serious compromises, and clear communication. Given our dysfunctional society, there may simply be no perfect solution for you, so do your best not to fall into the trap of guilt. It's important to come to the best solution you can and be with your child and focus on him as much as possible.

Stacey Tantleff-Dunn and husband Michael Dunn, both parenting experts and associate professors of clinical psychology at the University of Central Florida, cite ongoing communication about who-does-what as the key to successfully combining careers and parenthood.

"When you choose to work and raise children, you choose a life of constant juggling," says Tantleff-Dunn. "And, like any great circus act, your success depends on getting in sync with your partner. We have found that keeping a sense of humor, frequently discussing our priorities and goals, and staying really flexible make the hectic working parent life not only tolerable but also truly enjoyable. We often reassess how things are going and brainstorm changes to make things better. It's not always easy, but it is always worthwhile.

"Without doubt, having two young children and two careers challenges us in ways we never even imagined, but staying focused on what really matters to us makes it all possible. Our house isn't always spic and span, and our careers aren't exactly in overdrive, but our children are healthy and happy, we are productive at work, and we wouldn't trade any of it!"[1]

YOUR PARENTING PRIORITY PLAN

To establish a healthy balance between family and work, you and your partner (or anyone else who's going to be deeply involved in child raising) need to look carefully at priorities and take concrete actions to organize your lives accordingly. Here's our five-stage Parenting Priority Plan:

1. Evaluate how your parental programming may be influencing your parenting priorities.

2. Choose a supportive and healthy work life that enables you to spend enough time with your child.

3. Factor in time for your health, well-being, and relationships.

4. Allocate tasks and roles, and agree on a realistic budget.

5. Plan for ongoing evaluation and review.

Evaluate Parental Programming

As you begin your plan, consider whether your current child-rearing priorities have been driven by dysfunctional aspects of your program, perhaps stemming from your parents' approach to raising young children. You might ask yourself:

- Did one or both of your parents seem to see their worth only in terms of their career and consider parenting a secondary activity?

- Did they appear clear about their roles within the family and happy in them?

- Did they seem to enjoy the process of being with their children, or did they seem to feel that they were making huge sacrifices?

- Did the person who earned the most income make the important family decisions?

• Did your parents put aside special time together?

• How much time did your whole family spend together, and when? What made these times fun or not enjoyable?

• Which of the values and parenting practices you inherited do you now consider valid, and which do you wish to discard?

CHOOSE A SUPPORTIVE WORK LIFE

In determining your true priorities around balancing work and family, assessing your child's needs, and choosing healthy work options for one or both partners, you may find the following information and suggestions helpful.

Your Child's Needs

The number of mothers with children under one year old entering the workforce is rapidly growing. In the United States particularly, some mothers take only four weeks' maternity leave (usually unpaid), which after the birth may leave them with as little as one week to bond with their child.[2] Studies show the majority of women would like to take some time off in the early months, or even years, to be with their child but are concerned about financial pressures.[3] In fact, once mothers start to bond with their babies, many vigorously search for ways to allow the process to continue.

Spending enough time with your infant to learn to respond to his cues and allow the attachment process to successfully take place is one of the most important ways of preventing your child from suffering from depression and other problems later on. Exactly when you can safely leave your child in the care of day-care or preschool providers is a subject of great debate and controversy. Although it's not always possible, ideally, mother and infant would be together most of the time for at least the first twelve months (some say eighteen or even twenty), after which a well-attached child can be carefully prepared for Mom's gradually increasing absence.[4]

Remember that it's not *your* fault that society imposes almost impossible choices on parents and feeling bad isn't good for you or your baby.[5] Working mothers of young children can take heart from a study by researchers at Charles Sturt University that suggests that a working mother who has a real commitment to her work and less anxiety about the form of child care she has chosen is more likely to have a secure infant regardless of how early she returns to work.[6]

Many parents are told, often by day-care providers, that it's best to start day care as soon as possible, since many children don't make as much of a fuss over being left in a stranger's care when young. The tragic truth is that being torn from their mothers prematurely simply interrupts the attachment process; because it is premature, infants may not display appropriate distress at separation. Yet, the wounds, while less visible, may be far deeper and longer lasting. Many studies show, for example, that children who experience early and extensive day care are at risk for developing aggressive and noncompliant behavior.[7] Scholar Stanley Kurtz points out, "Low-level depression is a lot harder to find and verify observationally than obvious classroom bullying, but that doesn't mean it's not there."[8] Even when the child seems resilient, psychic injuries that are caused by too early separation can show up many years or even decades afterward.[9]

In the early months, it's not just a matter of *how much* time, even "quality" time (a concept given to us by marketing gurus in the child care industry to assuage maternal guilt), but of *when*. Forming a secure bond doesn't always happen according to the mother's work schedule, which can't take into account the periods when a baby is most open to stimulation and learning (usually in the morning), milestones such as saying a first word or seeing a first bird, or those times he needs a mother's reassurance and response *right then* so he knows he can count on it later.

Separation is painful for the mom as well as child. "My one-year-old still throws her arms around my legs and begs me not to go to work every single morning," one depressed, full-time executive told us. "Her cries echo inside my head all day. I thought it would get better for both of us as time passed.

But it's just gotten worse for me, especially when I think of her growing up, much of which I missed."

One mistake working mothers of infants often make is to unconsciously shield themselves from the pain of parting by dulling themselves to their infants' emotions. This process, called "desensitizing," interferes with a mother's ability to pick up on the baby's cues.[10] Mother's sensitivity is perhaps the most important factor in developing social competence and getting along with caregivers and teachers.[11]

Remember that your child's primary caregiver needn't necessarily be Mother—Dad, a relative, or other constant caretaker can also form a secure attachment. The next best alternative to one full-time attachment figure is time-sharing with your partner or other trusted caregiver. When early day care is inescapable, it's important to find a warm and supportive environment with a high caretaker-to-child ratio. (See Chapter 17 for more advice on choosing appropriate child care).

After infancy, if your child is secure, working at least part-time may have benefits for both of you. Some studies show that working mothers of older children are more likely to use authoritative parenting styles, characterized by explanatory communication, rather than less functional authoritarian or permissive ones, and that their children tend to be more socialized, well behaved, and intelligent. Also, working mothers tend to model competence, autonomy, and independence, particularly to their girls.[12] In our role as corporate consultants, we've found that top executives who receive training in communication skills and empathy at work use these same techniques to great effect with their families as well. Of course, your six-year-old still needs plenty of time with you.

While tons of research has shown that parents' work satisfaction affects their home life, one recent study showed the reverse to be true as well: children's moods and temperament significantly impact parents' sense of competence at work.[13]

Tip: If you are a working parent, allow pleasant thoughts about your child during the day, rather than blocking them in order to "compartmentalize" work and family. This will help you feel more connected to him when you get home.

Family-Friendly Work

If you have a choice about where you work, try to find a family-friendly workplace in which parents' needs are taken into account. The good news is that more and more companies are prepared to help, either formally or informally. A 2004 survey by the accountancy firm Deloitte Touche Tohmatsu found that that the number of U.S. firms that offer flexible hours increased from 50 percent in 2002 to 75 percent in 2004. During the same period, employees' desire to work flexible hours had increased from 65 percent to 82 percent. The feeling that one has control over work hours and schedule has consistently been associated with less work-family conflict, stress, and burnout.[14]

Working from home creates additional demands, such as your child expecting you to be with him if you're nearby, but it can be the best available solution if you want to earn supplemental income or keep your foot in the door of your career field, make contacts, and yet be with your children. Caution: part-timers often complain that they wind up having to do nearly as much work as full-timers, but at least they have more choice about when.

California's *Sacramento Bee* newspaper, furniture manufacturer Mitchell Gold Company in North Carolina, and Canada Post are among the 3 percent of major North American companies who offer child care facilities on-site for their staff. Those that have done so have found the exercise not only good public relations but also good for the bottom line—a fact you might mention to your employer. Companies are finding that they can save money and retain employees by allowing employees to time-share or work from home and telecommute rather than training replacements. In general, the most family-friendly sectors are technology, media, telecommunications, and financial services.

Other work opportunities include home-based businesses, franchises, consulting, Web design, real estate, tutoring, freelance writing, and translating. Most people have a skill that can generate income from home. Don't underestimate the potential pool of business experience and ideas of women you may meet in Lamaze classes and mothers' groups. One Australian environmental scientist hooked up with a New York marketing expert while waiting in her pediatrician's office, and the result was an internationally successful line of gourmet food products from the Australian bush.

Home and Work Transitions

Here are some suggestions for managing the transition between home and work:

- If you work for a company, review not only their parenting policies but also their mission statement or company credo. If the latter indicates a more liberal approach to the existing parental leave, child care, or flexitime policies, consider how the flexible work arrangements you want can be arranged.

- Deciding to take time off doesn't mean cutting yourself off from your industry or professional stimulation. Make sure you keep your business contact list current and schedule meetings or social get-togethers with work friends and new contacts.

- Upskill from home with correspondence courses—as long as it's material that really interests you and you have reasonable expectations about the availability of time and mental energy.

- If you work from home, set up a clearly defined workspace and enforce clear boundaries with older kids.

- If you possibly can, find a compatible person or people to go into business with. We all tend to work better in teams, and there will be someone to pick up the slack when you have to attend to your child.

Relationships at Work

When it comes to your child's well-being, as well as your own, the greatest factor at work is your relationships. Parents who report high levels of social support from coworkers and supervisors have greater job satisfaction, which correlates to a happy home life.[15] On the other hand, a stressful, unsupportive workplace can lead directly to a disempowered, harassed parent and a depressed child.[16]

"When I had a boss who constantly criticized me and clients who felt free to do the same, I'd come home tired and frustrated, and in spite of my best intentions I'd be irritated with my three-year-old Aidan and even my partner, Jason. The results were an unhappy, clingy, and tantrumy kid, and poor communication with Jason," says one mother. "When I started working with people who were really supportive and friendly, I came home happy and able to be more patient and attentive. Aidan's mood and behavior improved dramatically."

Although many working parents believe that they should keep family difficulties to themselves so as not to be seen as asking for special treatment, maintaining open communication with colleagues makes a big difference. "We all want to be there for Janet, and we understand her young child is having some problems," one senior partner at a high-profile consultancy firm told us recently. "But we need her to let us know where she needs help professionally and what's going on at home, so we can take that into account and cut her some slack."

> **Tip:** Take time to get to know your coworkers and be honest about any difficulties you may be having, including those related to child rearing. You'll probably find colleagues who are eager to share their own parenting joys and challenges.

FACTOR IN PARENTAL WELL-BEING

It's vital for your children's well-being, and your family as a whole, that you don't allow your own health and happiness to suffer. Be sure to include a large dollop of pleasurable, stress-busting, and healthy activities in your Parenting Priority Plan. Ask yourself how much time you need to spend on these activities, including:

- **Quality time for each other.** In trying to balance outside work and family, often the greatest casualty is time with your partner for something other than going over to-do lists. Being able to count on each other's love and support is the cornerstone of success in all areas, and it's important not to allow anything to get in the way. Plan time to really talk, even if it's only for a half hour a day, and make sure you keep up some activities you've always enjoyed together, from nature walks to a romantic dinner in or out. Above all, don't let those loving rituals slip: the parting kiss before leaving for work; shared meals; saying "I love you" at the end of each phone conversation; or playing like kids yourselves.

- **Quality time for yourself.** Just as important as quality time with your partner is allowing yourself to do the things you want to do (or to do nothing) rather than just what you feel you *have* to do. Taking quality time for yourself isn't selfish, it reduces stress in the household and ensures it isn't passed on to your children.

- **Friends.** Allow time to be with friends you can really talk to, especially same-gender friends. Too often parenthood leads to being cut off from those you used to rely on, particularly if they don't have kids the same age as yours. That is a great pity, because trusted friends are an essential release valve and sounding board. It is simply not possible to bring up a well-adjusted child without a good nexus of support around you. Isolated, a new mother, or even one having her second or third child, is almost bound to fall into a depressed state. If you are going to be a stay-at-home parent, it's vital you don't make home your prison. Avoid isolation by joining or starting a social or playgroup and catching up with friends in child-friendly environments such as libraries, bookstores, and parks.

- **Exercise.** Make sure you allow time for exercise, particularly walking. Exercise reduces your stress level and can be a powerful buffer against depression, including postnatal depression. Allow for at least a twenty-minute walk a day. You can take your baby with you very comfortably in a sling or baby carrier, which has the additional benefit of allowing close contact. Look for yoga or gym classes with an onsite crèche or children's play area or even a mommy/baby exercise class.

- **Nature.** Take time to experience nature, preferably with your family. At least once a week, walk in a park, go to the beach, or engage in any activity that gets you away from concrete and high-rises.

- **Meditation.** Allow daily time for meditation. Just fifteen minutes twice a day can made a big difference in how you cope with stress, which will help enormously in preventing your child from becoming depressed.

> **Tip:** Schedule these activities into your calendar and make sure you stick to them or they won't happen.

Allocate Tasks, Roles, and Budget

Before having a child, both men and women are often highly unrealistic about the real tasks and responsibilities involved and how they will respond.

When your infant is young, Dad's greatest job is to support Mom (if she's the primary caregiver), although later he has his own vital role to play directly with the child. Studies show that, while fathers' increasing help allows women to spend more time with their children, most fathers don't share the chores equally, even when mothers work full-time. In a Rowntree Foundation study, psychology professor Charlie Lewis of the University of Lancaster found that although most men said that they would share child care responsibilities if their wives were working full-time, in practice only 35 percent of fathers come anywhere close to equal participation.[17] Today's fathers spend on average 2.3 hours a day taking care of their young children's physical needs, compared to the 5.9 hours reported by mothers,[18] and logistics and transportation nearly always fall to the mother.

"Most men think being a house husband will involve popping in a bit of washing, taking the kids to school, and then putting their feet up with a cup of coffee," says Cary Cooper, an occupational psychologist and professor at the University of Manchester. "They are crazy. Housewives do much more multitasking than almost any man ever has to do in the workplace."[19]

Reaching Agreement

Since more couples fight over who does what than anything else except money, agreeing on roles and committing to them is essential to a harmonious and smoothly functioning household. First, decide exactly what needs to be done and who is available to do it. Then discuss what you each enjoy the process of doing. If neither of you want to do a certain task, consider (1) whether it really *has* to be done (perhaps let the lawn grow and call it a meadow) or (2) outsourcing it (cheaper in the long run than medical bills for stress-related illness).

This brings us to another important part of your Parenting Priority Plan—short- and long-term budgeting. This is one task you absolutely must share, or one of you may wind up frustrated and the other feeling controlled. You may find making the investment of time now in your young child requires cutting back on lifestyle, making financial decisions even harder. Having thought through your priorities should provide a firm guideline. Chapters 8 and 17 provide additional strategies for prioritizing and allocating roles and making decisions about child care.

When Adele, a top lawyer and executive coaching client of Alicia's, became pregnant with her second child, she was torn between her children's need for a constant caretaker and her desire to maintain the career she enjoyed and had worked so hard to attain. After working on their Parenting Priority Plan, Adele and her husband Paul decided that he would leave his full-time IT job, which he found stressful and demanding, for a part-time position as an on-site technical advisor at a local school. This would still enable them to afford a good nanny and allow him to spend afternoons with the children. Adele reported that the strategy worked well, and both parents and children seemed happy.

Tip: How much money is it OK to spend without consulting your partner? Agree on a fixed amount and be sure to discuss any purchases over that amount.

PLAN ONGOING EVALUATION
AND REVIEW

You'll probably want to keep a written record of agreed decisions regarding your Parenting Priority Plan, particularly what's most important to both of you, tasks, and budget. Along with activities that ensure your well-being, these agreements will shape your household routine (remember that consistent routine gives children security). Stick to your plan unless circumstances change, some aspects aren't working, or you think of better options. When you do make an alteration, make sure you both agree to it. It's a good idea for all caregivers to meet regularly and review how well the plan is being followed and what could be improved.

However you arrange work and family life, there are going to be problems and conflicts. The Dunns have a neat way of dealing with them. As Stacey says: "We often get through really hectic, difficult times by remembering that many of the problems that come up are short-term but how we handle them can have long-term effects on our family."[20]

6

STEP 3:
BUILD A NEXUS
OF SUPPORTIVE
RELATIONSHIPS
AROUND YOURSELF
AND YOUR CHILD

⊙

The linchpin of your success as parents is the quality of the relationships between yourselves as well as with your child. Study after study shows that marital satisfaction and, particularly in the early stages, the father's support of the mother as she bonds with her infant, are the keys to the child's lifelong optimism and emotional health.[1]

Siblings (especially older ones), extended family, caregivers, family friends, and work colleagues all play a vital role, first in supporting the new mother and, as the child gets older, as role models and part of the child's overall support system. Hence the often-quoted Kenyan adage "It takes a village to raise a child." Of course, for single parents, this extended support system is particularly crucial. You can enlist the people around you to help re-create the nurturing essence of the hunter-gatherer band, that unit that for two and a half million years prevented endogenous (long-term) depression among humans.

HEALTHY INTERDEPENDENCE

Sadly, modern humans seem to have lost the knack of forming truly supportive relationships. In fact, according to the World Health Organization (WHO), 80 percent of all relationships fail, a statistic further supported by a 50 percent divorce rate.

One problem is that society—like the "avoidant" infant who feels rejected by her mother and so, pitifully, tries to show that she no longer needs her—lauds self-reliance, independence, "pulling oneself up by the bootstraps," and "getting on with it." Self-help gurus call on us to find happiness within and to somehow "choose" not to be affected by the behavior of others.

All of this, of course, is nonsense and goes against the very essence of our humanity. The more intelligent the mammal, the less independent or instinct-driven she is at birth, and the longer she has to rely on Mom and the herd while she learns the ropes. Humans spend 20 percent of our lives as dependent children or adolescents, compared to 5 percent for most other mammals.[2]

In a seeming paradox, healthy self-reliance as an older child and adult depends on how much we were able to rely on our mother to be there for us in infancy and early childhood. If we were forced into an early separation by, for example, a preoccupied or rejecting mother, divorce, or early child care, we may become too outwardly self-reliant and unable to make healthy relationships. If we didn't learn early on that we could count on help when we really needed it—that the ideals were responsive to our needs—the resulting frustration and insecurity compromised our ability to seek appropriate goals, overcome challenges, and achieve the mastery that engenders optimism.[3] If, on the other hand, our mother did not encourage us to explore the world and instead kept us dependent for too long, we are liable to become clingy and unable to contribute meaningfully to any partnership, at work or home.

Studies have shown that emotionally healthy people, ones who were both self-reliant and able to rely on others (such as American astronauts), had home lives where both parents were loving and emotionally generous and their mothers had given them a feeling of complete security.[4]

One study found that the women who coped best with the demands of pregnancy and motherhood were those comfortable with relying on others.

They readily sought their husbands' support, asked directly for what they needed without hints or manipulations, and had the capacity to give spontaneously to others, including their babies. Women who fared less well either did not ask for support or did so in demanding, aggressive ways, perhaps due to their lack of confidence that it would be given. Typically, they were dissatisfied with what support they received and not competent at giving it to others.[5]

NEEDS-BASED DIALOGUE

The secret of successful relationships is to be clear about what you need from others (as the happiest mothers in the study above were) and what they need from you. In fact, we define relationships as the mutual satisfaction of need. However, most people don't state their needs clearly and directly; rather, they use manipulation and hinting, which force the other person to try to second-guess what is wanted, and this often fails. Many unarticulated needs that form the basis of relationships are dysfunctional, such as "I need you to control me" or "I need you to know what I want without my asking." These needs are based on negative aspects of the program and help perpetuate them. Identifying and expressing your needs clearly helps you spot and counter your inner saboteur—and that of others as well.

Most of our clients and students find it difficult at first to work out their real relationship needs. It's not as easy as it might sound. We all think that we know what we want; we have some vague, generalized ideas. But when it comes to translating these generalizations into concrete action-speak, we get stuck.

For example, we might say to someone "I need you to respect me." Respect is a feeling, and nobody can feel something on request. Neither can someone have a belief or thought on command. That is why saying "I need you to accept . . ." or "I need you to believe . . ." or "I need you to understand . . ." is pointless. Whether you're talking to your child, partner, babysitter, or friend, work out what you want them to *do or not do*, what *action or inaction* you want them to take, and ask for that.

Tanya and Toby were excited and nervous before the birth of their first child. After attending the Uplift Program, they used Needs-Based Dialogue®

to meet this new challenge. Each wrote down what they needed of each other, family, friends, and coworkers. The couple then expressed their needs to each other.

Tanya's needs of Toby included that he:

- Attend Lamaze classes with her before the birth.

- Take two weeks off around the birth date, and support her by attending the birth.

- Prepare the guest room for Tanya's sister, who was flying in to help for a few weeks, and make sure her sister had everything that she required.

- Serve as gatekeeper with his own parents, who tended to be controlling and critical, by telling them not to arrive until after the birth, arranging for hotel accommodations for them upon their arrival, and making it clear that they were not to criticize any aspect of his wife's mothering.

- Take turns comforting the baby at night.

- Not initiate sex and be willing to interrupt intimacies when the baby cries.

- Hold her and reassure her when she gets worried and upset from stress, fatigue, or hormonal imbalances.

Toby, in turn, gave a Needs List to Tanya, asking her to:

- Tell him immediately if she needs anything else.

- Lie down to rest, with or without baby, at least two hours a day.

- Tell him daily that he is important to her, even when she's focused on the baby.

- Take at least an hour a day to be alone with him without her sister, friends, or relatives around.

Tanya's needs for her sister while she was helping out included that her sister:

- Not make negative comments about Toby's pragmatic rather than perfect housekeeping.

- Make Tanya healthy snacks to keep up her energy levels.

- Give the couple time alone for an hour a day.

- Intercede with other family members and friends by answering questions and assuring them all was well.

For the most part, they each agreed easily to meet the other's needs, but in some cases they negotiated and made adjustments. Toby asked Tanya to let him get up and care for the baby when she cried at night since Tanya would be exhausted after the birth. Tanya said she would try to sleep, but if she was awake anyway she'd rather attend to the baby herself. Toby agreed.

Clearly stating their needs ensured that the birth and weeks afterward went as smoothly as possible, and baby's arrival was a joyful time for all. Of course, the three adults had more extensive needs lists for each other governing ongoing aspects of their relationships as well.

More informally, Tanya and Toby told their friends that they needed them to:

- Only call the house once after the birth to find out how the new family was doing.

- Call and arrange to visit mother and child starting one week after the birth.

- If they were good friends, arrange to visit Tanya weekly, during the day if possible, and go for a walk with her and the baby.

How to Use Needs-Based Dialogue

Tanya and Toby used our four-step model for Needs-Based Dialogue:

1. Identify your functional needs by making sure they meet our four basic criteria, fit under our four categories, and are allocated a priority zone. You may want to write these in a Needs List.

2. Express these needs to others.

3. Encourage others to tell you what they need of you.

4. Discuss the needs, saying which ones each of you will meet or not. Where possible, negotiate. Keep a written record of needs you both agree to meet.

IDENTIFYING YOUR NEEDS

We recommend that you write a complete Needs List for the important people in your life, including children over age three. Remember that these needs are about relationships, about what you need others to do or not to do. They are not a to-do list for yourself or a vague request of the universe, such as "I need more money."

Although later you will share these needs with the people they apply to, do this process on your own first so you won't be influenced by their ideas. Remember: not all needs are functional. For instance, "I need you to agree to everything I say" is not the basis for a good relationship, but "I need a veto over all decisions concerning the relationship" is. In order to be sure that a need is a relationship-enhancer, make sure that each need fits the four criteria and falls into one or more of the four categories listed here.

Tip: For important people such as a partner or best friend, aim to write ten needs under each category.

Four Criteria

1. **Concrete.** Needs should be specific and not general, often including instructions explaining how often, when, and in what way.

2. **Action-oriented.** Needs should be about doing or not doing. They should not be about feeling, thinking, understanding, or accepting. These are all emotions and cognitions that can't be measured or done on command.

3. **Doable.** Don't worry about if the specific person you're giving a need to can comply, but whether a person in her circumstances could. (Your mother may say she can't stop giving her unasked opinion about how you raise your child, but it is possible for mature human beings to refrain from doing so.)

4. **Appropriate.** Needs must be appropriate to the relationship. It was appropriate that Tanya ask her sister to give her time alone with her husband, and her sister accepted it as such.

Four Categories

1. **Physical safety.** Examples of needs under this category include those around money (Tanya needed Toby to postpone the search for his "ideal," though less highly paid, job as a landscape gardener and continue with his job at General Motors until she was ready to go back to work); needs that involve health (Toby's need that Tanya rest two hours a day); and needs that surround other aspects of safety, such as locking the doors at night.

2. **Emotional security.** This often involves trust issues, such as doing what you say you will and telling the truth.

3. **Attention.** Toby's need that Tanya spend an hour with him a day falls under this category.

4. **Importance.** Toby's request that Tanya tell him daily how important he was to her reinforced for him that he still had a significant role to play even when she was focused primarily on establishing the bond with her baby.

Priority Zones

Just because you give someone a need, or they give you one, doesn't mean it has to be agreed to. Saying no to a need and/or negotiating a compromise are both important aspects of Needs-Based Dialogue. In order to decide which needs are most important, which you can compromise on, and which you can't, it's helpful to assign them a colored "zone." These zones are, in ascending order of importance, green, orange, and red.

- **Green zone.** Green needs are basically wants or wishes. Tanya would like Toby to rub her back for fifteen minutes each day, but he could also massage her feet or even just hold her. Green needs are usually about attention, and there are many different ways to meet them.

- **Orange zone.** Orange needs are one step up in importance from green ones, but they are still somewhat flexible and open to negotiation. For instance, the couple asked their good friends to see Tanya weekly after she had a chance to rest, but if a friend is involved in a particularly critical work project or is traveling and makes arrangements to see her later, they will understand.

- **Red zone.** Responding to Tanya's need, Toby has told his mother that she is not to criticize how his wife handles their child. If Toby's mother continues to upset Tanya by doing so, she will be asked not to visit again. Breaking a red zone need damages the relationship, sometimes irreparably.

NEEDS WORK!

Although just thinking through what you need from the people in your life is very powerful in understanding yourself and countering the negative program, it is only the first step. If you want to get your needs met, you have to let people know what they are. Many people find this scary at first. "But they'll think I'm too needy!" they cry. Or, "They'll hear it as criticism or control." Or, "They won't meet them anyway!"

All of these objections usually melt away as people get up the courage to start communicating in these terms and experience the closeness and mutual understanding that results. However, let's look at these objections. As we've seen, humans are interdependent and thus "needy" by nature. In fact, if someone criticizes you as being "too needy" or tries to make you feel guilty for asking, they are trying to control you.

Telling someone what you need is simply a statement about you, not them. If they hear that as criticism or control, it's not your fault. Usually people come to see that Needs-Based Dialogue has advantages for them as well, especially once they understand that they can say no, negotiate, and give their own needs.

You'll probably find that those who want a mutually empowered relationship with you will be relieved to know in precise terms what they can do for you and what you expect from them and delighted to do what they can. People are naturally supportive; cooperation and altruism are in our genes.[6] We get a neural happiness reward when we help someone or when we meet their needs, and we feel upset when we can't or when we don't understand what they want of us.[7] We get a similar reward when someone meets a need we've given.

BOUNDARIES VERSUS BARRIERS

Expressing your needs appropriately creates boundaries that allow you and your child to be closer to others, rather than barriers, which create distance.

If you say to three-year-old Jenny "I need you not to run and shout in the hall," you are not only making a request of her, you are setting a boundary in place. The subtext of what you're saying is: "The best way for you to have a relationship with me is not to run and shout in the hall." Every need you give is a relationship statement, no matter whom you give it to. If you say to your partner "I need you not to contradict me in front of the children," you are setting a clear boundary within the relationship. If she doesn't agree to your request, or agrees and continues to undermine your authority with the kids, she's saying, in effect, "I will not respect your boundaries."

Unlike barriers, boundaries are not fixed and impermeable. Your needs change as you do, and they vary with the company you keep. Boundaries enable you to have relationships and to feel safe enough to do so. Barriers, on the other hand, keep people away and are more rigid and dysfunctional.

GUIDELINES FOR EXCHANGING NEEDS

There are many ways to give people needs and ascertain what they need of you, and how you do so will depend on circumstances and the nature of the relationship. You can give a need spontaneously at any time, such as when someone has transgressed your boundaries, perhaps criticizing you or not doing something they agreed to do. (The needs here might be phrased: "Criticism is not an appropriate way to speak to me and I need you not to criticize me." And "I need you to do what you say you will.") In order to get over a resistance to using what we sometimes jokingly call the "N-word," we often suggest that people use any excuse at all to do so, such as telling a shopkeeper or tollbooth attendant "I need a receipt."

In close and important relationships, such as with a spouse, good friend, or colleague (we'll talk about kids in a minute), it's a good idea to give needs in a more structured way. This involves first writing down your own needs and asking them to do the same. If they haven't read this book, or *Creating Optimism*, you may have to explain the rationale behind needs (to bring people closer together and enhance the happiness and effectiveness of each) and the criteria and categories. Don't forget to tell them that they can say no to any need or suggest negotiation. One man we know forgot to tell his partner that and then was puzzled when she didn't want to talk about needs. Who would, if you thought they were all nonnegotiable commands? However, of course, if someone won't accept your conditions for a relationship, especially your red zone needs, there will be consequences.

Let the other person know you are serious about this process and feel that it will help make your family, workplace, or friendship the best that it can be. Tell them when you would like to meet to begin the process of exchanging needs, and make sure they know you expect them to bring their Needs List of you. We've noticed that without a firm deadline this process often tends to get put off . . . and off.

It may take a few meetings to go through your needs. We suggest that each of you read out a need or two in turns and ask the other person to tell you if she understands the need and can meet it. It's important that you come out of the process with a list of agreed-to needs that you both can refer back to. Perhaps assign one person to write the agreements down and then copy them for the other. Once you've finished your Needs List, agree to meet regularly to discuss whether you each are doing what you agreed to and if new agreements are required. Put these dates in your calendar and stick to them! (For a more detailed description of giving needs in different situations, see *Creating Optimism*.)

Tip: Needs Lists are not just for people who are currently in your life. Writing a list of needs for an ideal support person, friend, or baby-sitter (or, for single parents, life partner and coparent) can be the first step in attracting additional supportive people into your life.

LISTENING TO YOUR CHILD'S NEEDS AND GIVING YOURS

Before your child can speak, she makes her needs known nonverbally by crying or reaching for things. You, in turn, show what you need by example, tone of voice, and consistency. For example, each time your baby pulls your hair painfully, gently remove her hand and say "no" firmly, but calmly. When she does something that pleases you, do things to let her know, such as smile and make delighted noises. Listening to a toddler's needs requires patience, as she won't always express herself either logically or clearly. You have to be a skilled interpreter, particularly of the under-threes. As the child grows up, she ideally learns to express what she needs concretely. In fact, children who feel their needs will be listened to are less likely to throw tantrums and display oppositional behavior, and the ability to communicate and negotiate emotional needs is a vital skill that enhances resilience.[8]

Parents sometimes neglect to verbalize requests or rules and may be inconsistent in applying them. "But surely they'd know not to do that!" is a common parental lament. Often children don't, or they are trying to get you to give clear boundaries. You must articulate your rules and expectations rather than expect your child to guess.

Be sure to express your needs and rules in concrete terms. Don't generalize. Don't say "be good," when you really mean "sit down at the table in your usual chair and don't throw food at your little brother!" "Be good" is a concept, and children under six don't understand such generalities (even adults disagree as to what they mean!).

As soon as your child begins to speak, it's very important to encourage her to ask clearly for what she needs. Listening to her needs is part of demonstrating empathy and making her feel she's a valued member of the band. If the need she gives is inappropriate, or if you can't meet it, say so. Don't criticize her for having a need by saying, "you shouldn't want that" or "you're too needy." Avoid putting her off by saying "maybe later," when you really know that "later" for this particular request probably won't happen. She can only learn to trust if she can count on you to tell the truth. Honesty is vital to consistency.

Adam and Jessica, former students of ours, made a point of encouraging their two-year-old Tess to be forthright with her needs. This made Tess a joy to be around, since she had far fewer temper tantrums than other kids of her age.

We witnessed the following interaction between Tess and Adam.

"Finger hurt!" she said, running into the room with tears in her eyes. "Daddy kiss finger!" Adam knew she hadn't seriously hurt her finger (no blood, no screams of pain) but that she was primarily expressing a need for sympathy and comfort. He could have dismissed her request or simply given her finger a quick peck, but that wouldn't have satisfied Tess's emotional need for him to listen to and acknowledge her problem.

"Show me where it hurts. How badly does it bother you?" Adam said, carefully examining the finger. He was showing that he cared about her finger just as much as she did, that she was important to him. "Do you want me to show you how to make it better?" Almost instantly the tears dried and curiosity took over.

Adam led Tess to the medicine cabinet and took out a Band-Aid. He showed her how to unwrap it and encouraged her to help him put it on her finger—"put it on where it hurts," he urged. To a child, the tiniest prick is a hole in the body that needs a Band-Aid to repair the leak.

When your young child expresses a need, apply the Needs-Based Dialogue rules in an age-appropriate way. Ascertain whether she has expressed a need that is doable and appropriate; if necessary, use simple explanations and negotiate by offering a limited range of choices.

One Saturday morning Jessica asked Tess what she would like to do. She replied that she wanted to go to the zoo and watch the seals (her favorite pastime) and also to have a picnic by the lake. Her mother knew that the distance between the two made it impossible to do both and still have time to see Tess's favorite animals. Jessica said: "Tell you what. Let's go to the zoo today and then to the lake next weekend." Tess was quite happy with this suggestion. She'd been heard; her opinion and her needs mattered.

How you relate to your partner is at least as important as how you relate to your child. Observing you and your partner candidly communicating your needs and setting functional boundaries will ultimately teach your child to do the same, enabling her to find safety and fulfillment in future relationships. The supportive nexus of people that she attracts will enable her to be resilient and optimistic and able to ward off depression.

STEP 4:
SET UP A CLEAR
PROCESS FOR FAMILY
DECISION-MAKING

⊙

Strolling in a mall the other day, we watched a brief interaction between a mother and her three-year-old son. She was obviously upset with something, and he had a reluctant expression on his face. They passed an ice-cream stand and the little boy tugged on her arm saying that she'd promised him a double chocolate cone "for being good." When she ignored him, he started to whine.

The mother grabbed him by the shoulders and shook him. "That's the second time you've asked! I warned you not to keep asking for things!" she said angrily. "I'll tell you when you can have something." Her son began to cry. A failure of communication, perhaps, but also something deeper and more significant.

The boy thought that an agreement had been made between them that he was going to get an ice-cream cone, presumably as a reward for going along with his mother's shopping expedition. She perhaps thought that she had the sole right to make such decisions and resented his demands. How dare a little boy of three have the right to hold his parent to her word and feel that his wants mattered!

The old adage that children "should be seen and not heard" is false and destructive. Feeling that you are in charge of your destiny—a sense of autonomy—is one of the major fundamentals of happiness, and it begins early. A child needs to feel both that his parents are in charge and in control of their lives and that his voice, his opinions, and his needs are heard and taken into account. Without that, defensiveness, pessimism, and depression are a real danger.

Adults often assume that children are incapable of making "rational" decisions; therefore, their opinions don't matter and parents have the sole right to decide what they should and should not want or need. Such a supposition couldn't be more wrong.

Consensus Decision-Making

Our remote ancestors had it right when it came to making decisions, and the few remaining hunter-gatherer tribes can teach us much about the process. When Bob lived among such a band of hunter-gatherers in southern Africa for about six months, he observed that all major decisions were reached by a consensus of adults. Anthropologist Colin Turnbull, who lived among the pygmies in central Africa in the 1960s, noted in his book *The Forest People* that a decision would often be delayed for some time until a consensus had been reached.[1]

Turnbull and others have observed that while children in these societies may not have a vote in important issues, they are brought into the decision-making process early. They are also given responsibility when young that equips them to play their role in the microdemocracy they live in. From the age of six or so, they are expected to plan their own hunting and foraging and make day-to-day decisions on a wide variety of matters concerning the economic life of the group.[2]

Bringing Children into the Decision-Making Process

Some parents are aghast when we advise them to take their kids into the family decision-making process. "My kids are too young to make decisions," they declare. Or, "What my kids say is cute but hardly relevant." In fact, research has shown that children from the age of one can, and do, make decisions and that problem-solving and good decision-making is a learned process that requires practice from a very early age.

According to Donna Mumme, assistant professor of psychology at Tufts University, "Babies are keen observers of other people and are able from a young age to gather information and make decisions. . . . Children as young as [one year] are making decisions based on the emotional reactions of adults around them."[3] A University of Iowa study found that preschoolers not only made choices based on weighing what they perceived to be in their best interests—both for the short-term and the long-term—but also that these decisions mirrored their parents' risk tolerance.[4]

Dalhousie University psychologist Nancy Garon found that children's decision-making abilities improved rapidly between age three and six and were closely linked to their temperamental characteristics—shy kids needed more encouragement in making decisions than extroverted ones—and their gender (girls were much better at making decisions).[5]

Obviously, your child can't be brought into the family decision-making process until he can talk coherently. "Dada" and "Mama" are probably not useful contributions to a "shall we move to Minneapolis" discussion. Even up to age six, his reactions are not based on adult reasoning, planning, or foresight, which he doesn't have yet to any degree, and his opinions don't have the same weight as those of the adults (he'll probably lose interest fairly rapidly anyway). But in order to encourage him to feel part of the family and elevate his sense of self-worth, he should be invited into the process from about age three.

Often we ask students, "Can you remember anyone inviting your opinion about anything when you were young?" Almost invariably the answer is "no." Parents are often too busy, too insecure in their own roles as parents, or too disempowered in other areas to take the time to draw out children's thoughts and ideas. A 2004 Rowntree Foundation report, "Young Children's Citizenship," emphasizes the need to "build participation into routine interactions between adults and children in everyday settings" such as the home, primary school, or kindergarten. The consequences of not doing so: children who grow up unable to make informed choices in areas such as politics, consumer affairs, drugs, media, or mates.[6]

Tip: To give your child practice in daily decision-making and keep it simple, offer him a choice between specific alternatives such as a fruit juice or yogurt when you're at the store. Don't ask him to figure out a generality, such as "something that is not too expensive."

THE FAMILY POWWOW

Since your family (including all who live with you or significantly participate in your lives, such as adult children, nannies, or close extended family) is a miniband or "tribe," it's useful to meet for regular meetings we call Family Powwows. (Kids love this Native American term.) The purpose of the powwow is to reach consensus on family decisions, solve problems, and (as we'll see in Chapter 8) determine household rules and roles. Often these issues are discussed first by the parents and adults who have ultimate responsibility for the others and the final say. We refer to this group as the Council of Elders.

During the Family Powwow, one member of the Council of Elders will act as chair of the meeting and another as secretary. It is important that your children see that these positions rotate and, therefore, don't develop hierarchical stereotypes. Obviously, not all decisions are convenient or appropriate for the powwow, but appropriate decisions can cover anything from where to go to kindergarten and what to do for family holidays to reviewing family budgeting issues. Try to discuss issues that concern the younger children first, because they will probably want to leave the discussion early. Everyone should be encouraged to have their say, though the final decisions should be made by consensus of the council.

Every family decision discussed at the Family Powwow should involve four stages:

Powwow Decision-Making Process

1. Define the problem and/or desired goal, using specific, simple terms that everyone can understand. Avoid generalizations.

2. Brainstorm all options. Make sure that each person states his or her case and is listened to seriously, even the youngest.

3. Select the best possible alternative, as a group. Try for consensus of all members, or else the decision reverts to the Council of Elders.

4. Follow through and implement the decision. Decide what actions are needed and who will take them, and schedule the next Family Powwow.

EMPOWERING ALL FAMILY MEMBERS

Powwows greatly minimize family tension and conflict, empowering all members and teaching them to be open, empathetic, and flexible. Because each person knows that his opinion is sought and valued, he will be more committed to the eventual decision. Research shows that families who use this consensus style of decision-making show improved family functioning, family satisfaction, self-esteem, and family coping levels, while reducing family strains, stress, and depression.[7]

The following tips will help make the Family Powwow most effective.

• Select a time for the powwow when all family members are fully able to participate.

• Require that all participants demonstrate respect for each family member, even the youngest, as an individual with his own rights and needs.

• Allow time for each person to express his ideas and suggestions. Be patient; it's a learning process for all of you.

• Teach all members to actively listen to others' points of view. Model this process by repeating what you think the other person said as well as checking to see if they understood what you said.

- Set realistic goals. Be sure the goals your family chooses are reasonable and can be met within your time frame. In order to avoid conflict, it's so easy for some member of the family to say "yes, yes" when they're really feeling "maybe, maybe" or "no, no."

- Address conflict calmly when it occurs. Don't avoid a topic just because it's contentious. If anyone becomes angry or upset, encourage him to talk about his feelings, but put off trying to solve the conflict until everyone can approach it in a positive and constructive way. If you're feeling out of control, stop. Don't start again until you are able to communicate calmly.

- Avoid criticizing, yelling, blaming, or name-calling. Make sure everyone understands that these behaviors are against the rules and won't be tolerated.

PUTTING FAMILY POWWOWS INTO PRACTICE

Ted and Marcie Rose have three children: Katie, twelve; Courtney, ten; and Timothy, five. Marcie was prey to depression for many years and was determined that her children would not suffer as she had.

Under Alicia's guidance, she put into practice many antidepression techniques for herself and her family, including the Family Powwow. "From the start of our marriage, Ted and I set aside a regular time to discuss any problems that we had, what our needs of each other were, and what joint approach we should take to issues like who we would visit over Christmas," she says.

"These meetings were always open, and as our children grew into toddlers they became curious. Often Katie would come and sit on my lap while Ted and I were having the meeting, so she'd get quite used to being there. She wasn't always quiet, of course, but she enjoyed being part of things. Courtney and Timothy joined the powwow in much the same way.

"The powwow is now a weekly family ritual, and Katie and Courtney will often bring lists of topics to discuss, decisions they want made, and needs of Ted and me. It's not that they don't bring issues up at other times; it's just that they know that at these get-togethers they will have our full attention and that when we've all agreed to something, it'll get done. Increasingly the girls' suggestions are really quite good and we adopt them. Even Timothy has had some great ideas, such as that the family have a games night on Sunday evenings. We stick a reminder of the agreements we've come to on the refrigerator with all of our signatures on it—even Timothy insists on putting on his scribble."

A FORUM FOR NEEDS

The powwow offers an opportunity to encourage each member of your tribe to present their needs to the rest of the group and to learn to respond appropriately to others' needs. A need isn't a command. Just because someone has a need doesn't necessarily mean that anyone has to meet it. Marcie says, "When one of us presents a need to the family as a whole that involves the rest of the family, everyone has a say. Just last week I said, 'I need you all to come with me to select a new sofa, since the one we have is getting very ratty.' The girls immediately agreed, but Ted said he felt that we couldn't afford a new sofa at present and therefore he didn't see the point.

"I said that it was important to me to have a presentable home. At this point, Courtney chirped in, 'Let's make a budget!' (*Budget* was a word she'd often heard her father use when he talked about his work or the household expenses.) Katie asked Ted how much we could afford, and before he had a chance to answer, Tim suggested a trillion dollars. (I'm not sure he knows what *trillion* means; it's a word he's picked up recently.) Ted told him that, generally, sofas don't cost that much, unless, of course, they are being bought for the military. Eventually we settled on $1,000. The agreement we all came to was: 'We'll all shop for a new sofa on the understanding that we'll only spend a maximum of $1,000.'"

No one laughed at Timothy for suggesting a trillion-dollar budget; rather, he was taken seriously, and because of that he won't be afraid to bring his ideas to the table in the future. His self-esteem will be enhanced by the way he was listened to and this in turn will increase his level of optimism.

In the next chapter, we'll give you more tips on how to use needs to establish rules the whole family will follow—plus putting in place two elements that are vital to the well-being of families but that are often overlooked: roles and rituals.

8

STEP 5:
ESTABLISH RULES,
ROLES, AND RITUALS

◉

A young child is the product of the nexus of relationships around her. She reflects the context of her parents, siblings, relatives, caregivers, family friends, and, to a lesser extent, the society she finds herself in. If that context is harmonious and optimistic, so in all likelihood will she be. If those within it are unhappy, angry, out of control, critical, or absent, she will reflect that as well.

The most important fundamentals of harmonious relationships are what we call the "three Rs": rules, roles, and rituals. Together, these form the glue that holds any social group together, be it a couple, family, nexus of friends, club or association, corporation, or society. Each of these must have agreed-upon rules of conduct, accepted roles for its members, and bonding rituals. Without these three Rs, any social unit will be effectively out of control, leading to its dissolution, a high state of depression or anxiety, and/or the rise of an abusive tyrant.

A violent, authoritarian father, or a dictator such as Adolf Hitler, is a product of an out-of-control family and is allowed to rule others because they—or a significant portion of the micro- or macrosociety—believe that their world is out of control. Children of such a family will most likely grow up to be depressed or bullies or both.[1]

Bjørn Grinde notes in his book *Darwinian Happiness* that "the brain is not born in its final form, but rather designed to mature by means of interaction with the environment."[2] Family rules, roles, and rituals are what regulate a child's environment and allow her brain to develop as it should.

HOUSE RULES

Not too long ago, Bob was asked to help a family in chaos. Naomi Thompson and her husband, Bryce, were constantly fighting. Both worked long hours: Naomi as a part-time librarian and home-based business owner and Bryce as a foreman at a large building firm. Their eight-year-old son, Cameron, lied to his parents and bullied his five-year-old sister, Miranda, who showed signs of depression, had difficulty making friends, and rarely did what she was told.

"What would you say are the rules of the house?" asked Bob at their first session. Naomi and Bryce looked at each other.

"You mean what rules do we lay down for the kids?" Naomi suggested.

"No. What are the rules that apply to all members of the household," Bob persisted.

"It's not us who need rules," said Bryce angrily. "It's not Naomi and I who are out of control."

Parents often mistakenly think that rules are just for the kids. They themselves, being adults, are in control and "just know" how to behave appropriately. Parents may feel that having household rules that apply to them is too restricting and would trap them, but just the opposite is true. Having a set of agreed upon rules can be liberating, because it adds to your security. No one can feel safe in any relationship if she does not know how the other person will react in various circumstances. Consistently applied rules also provide a sense of boundaries and thus safety in the family. They allow a child to develop a strong sense of inner control and thus not need to be controlling in later relationships.

Bob soon discovered that Bryce was authoritarian, with a "What I say goes" approach to discipline. Yet because he was not consistent, and his rules and enforcement depended on his mood or whim, they weren't obeyed, and the children couldn't feel safe.

Even Bryce and Naomi weren't consistent or clear with each other, often resulting in accusations such as "you should've known" and "but you never said!" Naomi seemed hesitant to enforce any rules at all, thus giving the kids even more confusing messages. The lack of clarity and boundaries in the household was reflected in the children's behavioral problems. Part of what keeps a child from being depressed is the sure knowledge of the rules and the consequences for breaking them. The Thompson kids had no clear idea of what was expected of them, except to be afraid of their father when he was angry. Since Bryce frequently criticized his wife, so did the kids. Bryce's son picked up his father's anger and took it out on his sister, the only one with less status than himself. Each sibling would blame the other for whatever went wrong—just as their parents blamed each other.

"How do we figure out what the rules are, or even what they should be?" Naomi asked Bob, ignoring the disapproving look from her husband.

Bob explained that successful relationships are built on the mutual meeting of needs and that when a family member gives a need to another member or to the family as a whole, and that need is accepted, the resulting agreement becomes a household rule. He stressed that these needs must be clearly expressed and agreed. Although Naomi and Bryce, as the responsible adults, had the final say, enforcing the rules would be much easier if they could get their children to buy into the process. On the face of it, this was a daunting task.

The couple agreed to try our simple, three-step process for reaching rules the whole family can agree to:

Establishing Household Rules

1. Exchange needs and agree on basic household rules. This exchange should be done between parents (and other members of the Council of Elders). Similar to the criteria for needs, rules must be concrete, action-oriented, doable, and appropriate. "Appropriate" is particularly relevant to rules in a household of many ages.

2. Discuss and negotiate rules with the whole family at the Family Powwow, making additions and adjustments. Keep a written list of house rules.

3. Enforce rules consistently with clear consequences, and review at regular powwows.

PARENTAL AGREEMENTS

The first step toward a more functional family is for the Council of Elders—in this case, the two parents—to get together and work out their needs of each other and some basic rules for the whole family. It was hard to get Bryce to even admit that he had needs, let alone say what they were. Eventually, however, he was able to communicate some basic needs to Naomi: "I need you to be faithful" and "I need you not to lie to me."

Bob asked Naomi whether she could agree to meet those needs, and she said she could. "OK," Bob said. "Those are the first rules of the relationship. Do you think the need about not lying can be extended to everyone in the household—is it a need you have of your children as well?"

"Of course!" Bryce said. "I've told them often enough!"

"But only in the same way that you've made some other demands that you didn't stick to," said Bob. "There's no way they can know what is a rule of the house and what is your whim. They may perhaps obey momentarily out of fear, but they won't respect any rule you make."

"That's true," said Naomi. "As soon as your back is turned, they do what they like."

By the end of the first session of the Council of Elders, the couple had written a list of rules that would be put to the first Family Powwow, including:

- No lying

- No criticism or put-downs of anyone, including family members and teachers

- No swearing

- No wearing dirty shoes in the house

- Keep your own room clean

ORDER IN THE HOUSE

At the first Family Powwow, Cameron became sullen when the rule of "no lying" was introduced. However, he perked up when assured the rule also applied to his dad, mom, and little sister, and he finally agreed. Both children lobbied for being able to keep their rooms as messy as they pleased. Naomi agreed, on the condition that no food was brought into the bedrooms and that the kids—and Bryce—picked up after themselves in common areas.

Five-year-old Miranda added a rule that shocked her parents: "No one hits anyone." It was the first glimmer that Bryce and Naomi had of the extent of Cameron's bullying. With Bob's help, Bryce realized his own harsh words and implied threat of physical punishment had contributed to his son's aggressive behavior. Naomi saw that leaving discipline to her husband had also played a part. Both became determined to ensure that a more structured, collaborative approach worked and would ultimately bring more harmony to their lives.

Tip: Post house rules on the fridge or blackboard.

ENFORCING THE RULES

As the famous behaviorist B. F. Skinner pointed out in a 1986 article called "What's Wrong with Daily Life in the Western World," there's no point in having rules without the willingness and a mechanism to enforce them.[3]

While children actually crave order, they may at first resist your instructions, if only to make sure that you stand firm in your parenting role and thus give them safety. Plus, both adults and children resist change. If you want to teach your kids that their behavior in the real world has consequences—such as that if they don't show up to work they probably won't get paid—you need to start demonstrating in a loving way that actions cause certain things to occur.

Like the rules themselves, consequences for breaking them should be discussed and, if possible, agreed to. They also must conform to certain criteria:

- Consequences must be consistently applied.

- Consequences must be appropriate to the behavior. This seems obvious, but harsh punishments are sometimes meted out for trivial offences.

- Consequences must apply to every family member, although they may differ. For example, the consequence for a child of breaking the "no swearing" rule might be missing a favorite TV show and for an adult donating $5 to the family vacation fund.

- Physical punishment is never appropriate. Slapping, shaking, hitting, caning, and strapping are all forms of physical abuse. An abused child may well become a depressed, abusive, or abuse-attracting adult.

- Verbal abuse is never appropriate. This includes criticism, belittling, or berating—any of which can lead to depression and a loss of self-esteem (in both adults and children).

- Denial of food should never be used as a punishment. (It is OK, however, to deny a child dessert if she doesn't eat dinner.) From very early in life, food and love are equated and the denial of food is the equivalent of the withdrawal of love.

Examples of nonharmful consequences for young children are: time-outs; denying TV programs, computer time, or electronic games; confining to the house for a period of time; canceling a play date or sleepover; or doing extra chores.

The powwow is the ideal forum for the family to sign off on consequences for transgressions as well as to agree to the rules. These decisions can and should be revisited at ongoing Family Powwows. Young children are actually very inventive—even overzealous—at coming up with consequences. Miranda suggested that if she came into the house with dirty shoes on "I should have to go always barefoot forever!" This was amended to having to sweep the floor afterward.

It took the Thompsons a few months to get used to the new order, and, of course, there were hiccups while the children tested the parents' resolve. But in the end, parents and children came much closer together, and the negative behaviors mostly stopped.

DEFINING ROLES

Having a role within the family or, indeed, any group is essential to a sense of belonging and importance. Without a clear role, anyone will feel in danger of exclusion and can become depressed.

Research by Dr. James Nazroo of the University College, London, and others has shown that belittling or denigrating a person's role in the family is one of the prime causes of depression, especially among women.[4] The risk of a depressive episode after a crisis involving one of a woman's traditional roles in the areas of children, housing, and reproduction was five times greater than if a man faced a crisis regarding one of his traditional roles, such as financial provision.[5]

According to one study, sports players who become uncertain about their role in their team lose a sense of belonging, self-esteem, and competence and become depressed.[6] According to research done by human development professor Elizabeth Vandewater of the University of Texas and others, well-defined, accepted, and appreciated roles not only give us security, they allow for the proper development of personality over the course of a lifetime.[7]

University of Central Florida psychology associate professors Stacey Tantleff-Dunn and her husband Michael Dunn worked out their roles consciously but not rigidly. "It was important to quickly recognize that partnership, even when fifty-fifty, did not mean that we each did half of everything," Stacey Tantleff-Dunn told us. "There were some things that Mike tended to do like taking out the trash or trimming the hedges, and other things that I routinely took care of like laundry and scheduling checkups, haircuts, and the like. I think that the key to our happiness was NOT keeping score, and remembering to value and appreciate each other's contributions to keeping our household afloat.

"Since Mike doesn't tolerate sleep deprivation very well and I seem to function on very little sleep fairly well, I always got up with the baby in the middle of the night, but then he took over so that I could rest in the morning. We rarely had to negotiate assigned responsibilities, but we made an effort to communicate our needs and look out for one another. That said, I can remember a few times when I felt overwhelmed, shortchanged, or unappreciated and 'communicated' in ways that weren't very effective. Mike wisely learned to cut me some slack and react to my inappropriately expressed needs rather than my words."[8]

Where the parents have a secure relationship and there is also a strong bond between parents and older children, roles often evolve naturally. In new situations (such as the birth of a child), where family members are still learning communication skills and establishing the decision-making process, the powwow can be an excellent forum for acknowledging and agreeing to roles and allocating respective tasks.

To be functional, roles must meet the following criteria:

• Clearly defined, with specific tasks, and as little overlap as possible (Does raking the lawn include sweeping the driveway?)

• Agreed to by all the family, especially the person who takes on the role (Roles can become a source of friction if one member of the family is given a role she's not happy with.)

- Where possible, reflective of the natural skill or competency of the person

- Acknowledged by everyone as important (There are no "minor" roles; each is significant, if only to the person carrying out the role. Praise must be given for doing whatever the role entails.)

- Sensitive to gender issues

Tip: Start a discussion about roles at the Family Powwow by asking everyone what they think their roles are at present and if they're happy with them.

FATHER'S ROLE IN MODERN FAMILIES

A father's traditional role is changing and is far more complex than before. Confusing expectations about his role in family life are leading to increasing stress and, in many cases, depression.

Recent research suggests, for example, that some men who take on the primary housekeeping role have an 82 percent higher death rate, mostly from heart disease.[9] In this role-reversal situation, particularly if a man feels he's being forced into an unwanted role, he can lose his self-esteem and become angry and resentful. As psychology professor Kathi Miner-Rubino of Western Kentucky University notes: "Men whose feelings of personal power, confidence, and identity are derived from the work role may feel at odds with leaving paid employment and, as a result, may begin to question 'who they are' and their personal worth."[10] This is not to say that men shouldn't do their share of household chores, just that nobody should be forced, through guilt or social pressure, into roles he or she feels are inappropriate.

The arrival of a first or even second and third child has a major impact on a father's role, as well as his relationship with his partner. In the often quoted article "The Father-Child Connection: A Struggle of Contemporary Man" in *Psychiatric Times*, UCLA psychiatry professor Robert Moradi wrote: "When the baby is born the father finds himself No. 2 or the outsider to both mother and baby. The love affair is between mother and child. Ashamed of his competition with the baby and feeling betrayed by his wife, he feels unloved, unacknowledged, and useful only for providing the needs of [mother and baby]. . . .

"If mourning the loss of how the relationship was with his wife, and awareness of the good aspects of becoming a father are not adequately provided for, the man will cope in familiar ways to survive the [emotional] assault. For instance, one man might work hard and unconsciously try to gain his wife back . . . by doing better and more of what he knows how; another man might give up and find solace in an affair or substances; yet another might compensate by creating his own 'baby,' e.g., building, inventing, producing, and expanding in the physical or spiritual world."[11]

Ideally at this stage, the father should offer uncritical support for his partner as she bonds with the baby, ask clearly what she needs, and spend extra time with older kids. If he hasn't already done so, he should decide which types of nurturing activities he wants to be involved in and how much time he wants to spend with each child (if changing diapers isn't for him, he should say so!). If he has chosen to be the primary caregiver for the child, it's vital that he has enough information and support from his partner, friends, and perhaps a parenting or father-child group. Whatever his role, he must insist his partner acknowledge and praise his efforts and not forget to maintain the loving rituals that bond the couple.

Later, taking an active and involved fathering role and providing watchful protectiveness over the child will, as Moradi reminds us, help a father become "more competent, have higher degrees of compassion for others, manifest fewer sex-stereotyped beliefs, and have a more solid internal locus of control." Furthermore, "within the emphatic connection learned by fathering, men have the chance to develop their own sense of mature masculinity."[12]

Tip: No one should agree to a role that they aren't comfortable with. Be honest and concrete about your needs around chosen roles.

ROLES AND RESPONSIBILITIES FOR YOUNG CHILDREN

It's appropriate for kids older than age three to have roles, and from the age of six these roles can even contribute to the family well-being or finances.

For example, eight-year-old Cameron proudly volunteered to take on the role of Mom's chief postal assistant for her part-time home business. He was put in charge of bicycling down to the local post box to mail letters and making sure there was enough petty cash to cover stamps. He took seriously this indication of trust and began to inform himself about the cost of other business expenses as well. Miranda begged to be in charge of sticking stamps on letters (her brother agreed) and zealously guarded her role, becoming quite frustrated if anyone else in the household put a stamp on an envelope! Naomi and Bryce explained how important budgeting and mailing letters was to the family's economic well-being and lavished praise on the enterprise.

One depressed young boy, who was physically slight and had been overshadowed by athletic older sisters, came out of his shell when his father gave him a role that was traditionally male and highlighted his son's natural skill. Noticing how much the boy enjoyed taking apart and putting back together his toys, his father nominated him "handyman's helper" and asked his son to help him fix things around the house by handing him the right screwdriver or other small tool. The boy's self-confidence—and his relationship with his father—both flourished.

Some other responsibilities for children under six could include the following:

- Setting the table

- Feeding pets dry food and water

- Fetching the newspaper

- Folding and putting away towels

- Putting toys away

- Laying clothes out

- Getting dressed (including brushing teeth and combing hair)

> **Tip:** "Chores" should not be classed as such but rather seen as part of unique roles. Chores will often be resisted, roles not nearly so much.

BONDING RITUALS

The last of the three Rs is rituals. The old phrase "a family that prays together, stays together" contains a lot of truth. Like all rituals, praying together increases the bonds among participants.

Most families have habits and customs, but these are often not true rituals. In his book *Secular Wholeness: A Skeptic's Path to a Richer Life*, David Cortesi explains what sets rituals apart: "An act becomes a ritual for you when you perform it with conscious awareness of its symbolic and emotional meaning, and with willing assent to those meanings. Unless you act with both awareness and assent, your act is merely a habit (if it is unique to you) or a custom (if you share it with others)."[13]

Since there is no functioning social unit without rituals, the need for them seems to be embedded in our genes. Recent studies by Dr. Barbara Fiese of Syracuse University found that rituals have enormous benefits, including increased marital satisfaction and mental and physical health. Children who grow up in families that have rituals develop a much stronger sense of self than those who do not.[14]

Faith-based rituals are, of course, very powerful and have been shown to create strong, resilient, and long-lived families. However, as Cortesi says, almost any aspect of family life can be turned into a ritual, provided the members agree. In *Drawing Families Together One Meal at a Time*, authors Jill and

Neal Kimball (together with Stacey Tantleff-Dunn and Michael Dunn) list a number of rituals that can evolve around shared meals. These include: lighting candles before a special meal; using family mealtime to celebrate events such as losing a tooth, scoring a goal, getting a new job, or passing an exam; taking turns choosing a dinnertime conversation topic; and creating dinners with a theme suggested by rotating family members.[15]

Rituals around meals seem to gain extra resonance when shared with extended family and friends, such as during Yom Kippur, Christmas, or Thanksgiving. But you don't have to wait for a holy day or holiday to invite nearby extended family and friends over for a meal—we set aside one evening a week to share an informal, often potluck, dinner with people we care about.

The three Rs—rules, roles, and rituals—bind a family together. In the next chapter, we'll look at how a simple habit can transform your entire family.

9

STEP 6:
CREATE A FAMILY
CULTURE OF
APPROPRIATE PRAISE

◉

Making a habit of praise has dramatic and ongoing payoffs for all family members. Praise benefits both the giver and the receiver. The receiver gets a boost to his self-esteem and, if commended for doing something well, his sense of competence. The giver gets an equally valuable reward: seeing the faces of those he cares for light up and strengthening a relationship. Both parties get a neurochemical happiness boost.

Yet the strange thing is that so very few families have a culture of praise. Parents often tell us that they try not to praise their kids too much so as not to give them an inflated idea of themselves. That is utter nonsense. What children *will* get if praise is withheld is a very low sense of self-worth and competence. Most of our depressed clients lacked praise and were criticized as children. Depression and pessimism just don't seem to grow out of appropriately praising households.

APPROPRIATE PRAISE

There are three different kinds of praise. Each is necessary at the right time and each can be damaging if it is the only type a child or adult receives.

1. Praise for achievement (what he does)

2. Praise for process (how he does it)

3. Praise for the person (who he is)

Praise for Achievement

Praise for achievement is the most obvious and frequently given type of praise. Whenever you think someone, especially your child, has done something well, tell him. It's from the praise of others that a person gets a sense of competence, one of the eight fundamentals of happiness. The downside of achievement praise can be if it's the only kind given.

Many top executives who crucify their family life and their own health on the altar of hard work and success were only praised as children for accomplishments, usually outstanding ones—learning to walk, getting straight As, winning at sports. They find it hard to comprehend that they have any intrinsic worth and are often driven by the terror of failure—which they see as anything less than dramatic success. These are the values they can't help but pass on to their children, coupled, if one or both parents work long hours, with the sense of abandonment. Others are so focused on the fear of failure that they never experience any success, and this trait too can be passed down the generations—along with accompanying depression.

Achievement praise loses its power if it's used indiscriminately—if, for example, "that's fantastic!" covers everything equally from finishing dinner to riding a bicycle alone for the very first time. This devalues the effort the child put into learning a difficult new skill. A 2003 study led by Professor Roy Baumeister of Florida State University showed that indiscriminate praise for achievement, far from raising good self-esteem, can actually "promote narcissism and its less desirable consequences," such as extreme self-absorption, the inability to make friends or behave appropriately in social situations, irrational anger at others, and a lack of interest in learning.[1]

Tip: Preschool-age children can take more praise for achievement than older kids, who tend to get more cynical.[2]

Praise for Process

Columbia University psychologist Carol S. Dweck has shown that what she calls "process praise"—for effort, inventiveness, keeping at it—is the most effective kind. When praising young students, for example, says Dweck, "You really have to appreciate what went into producing what the students produced: what went into the ideas, the strategies, the choices, the development, the execution of the project."[3]

Process praise is not focused on outcomes, yet it helps children actually do better at tasks. If a child gets praise for trying hard, even though he only got a C, he is more likely to get a better mark next time.[4] He also learns that *how* he does something is important. He will keep using the techniques and ways of thinking that he got praised for and that are most likely to bring about a sense of mastery and success—both major factors in preventing and healing depression.

Tip: Ask your child why he did something a certain way and then praise the process. Adult: "How come you drew all those windows in the house?" Child: "So we can see the trees and birds." Adult: "What a great idea!"

Praise for the Person

Bob is constantly praising Alicia for just being her, for just being the person she is. It's reciprocated, and this kind of praise is an integral part of their relationship.

People need to know that they're valued just because of who they are, without having to strive for this recognition. Bob will frequently say, "I'm so lucky I found you! You're wonderful." In the same way, you can say to your child, "You're a great kid." This is relationship-cementing praise par excellence! But it's also a statement about your feelings toward your child. The subtext is: "I love you and I'm not going to abandon or desert you." Since, as we've seen, there's nothing a child fears more than abandonment, this is a vital ongoing reassurance.

Tip: Notice how often you praise family members for just being who they are. Try to make sure you do so at least once a day.

BAD PRAISE

Surprisingly, there is bad praise. Dweck and colleague Melissa Kamins note that using general, nonspecific praise in order to help your child to do better at something can lead to "vulnerability and a sense of contingent self-worth." Just telling a child he's "good" when you're really pleased he's picked up his toys doesn't let him know specifically how he can maintain your approval.[5]

Even praising a child for a fixed trait such as intelligence or being musical or athletic can backfire. The child has no control over these genetic characteristics.

Says Dweck: "Praising children's intelligence, far from boosting their self-esteem, encourages them to embrace self-defeating behaviors, such as worrying about failure and avoiding risks." In fact, when you're trying to use praise to reinforce certain behaviors, praising the child for set traits can have the same negative effect as criticizing him for factors beyond his control.[6]

Dweck found that labeling children as gifted or talented may also have a negative impact by causing them to become overly concerned with justifying that label. They may become less willing to risk academic setbacks by taking on challenges that enhance their learning and mastery skills.[7]

PRACTICING PRAISE

A culture of praise helps promote a general sense of harmony within the household (or within the school or corporation). In his book *The Marriage Clinic*, John Gottman talks about the "emotional bank account" and the "fondness and admiration system" that allow a couple to draw on "stores" of good feelings that have been deposited there by each partner. A good ratio of positive to negative interactions (at least five to one) predicts a satisfying relationship.[8]

In establishing a family culture of praise, it's not enough just to show approval of your children; all family members must praise each other. The younger ones will idealize and take on the praising behavior of the older children and adults, and everyone's sense of security will be strengthened because it is clear that no one is being rejected.

Of course, that means that you have to get used to receiving praise as well as giving it—something that is very difficult for many in our society. Think of ways to praise your partner several times a day and ask your partner to do the same for you. If praising doesn't come naturally to one of you, here are some examples:

- Congratulations on getting that new account!

- I noticed that you didn't lose your temper with the kids but used time-outs. Well done!

- I love living with you.

Tip: Practice praising as many people as possible. You'll be pleasantly surprised at the results! Praise the guy at the fish counter if the catch is particularly fresh; tell the preschool teacher something nice your child said about her; find something positive to say about your best friend or colleague every time you get together.

NEVER CRITICIZE

According to the American Academy of Pediatrics, "belittling, degrading, or ridiculing a child is a major cause of depression.[9] Yet it's amazing how few people realize the damage that criticism does to individuals within the family and the unit as a whole. Whenever we speak about criticism at corporations or in courses or the media, someone always asks, "But what about *constructive* criticism?" There's simply no such thing. All criticism is about control, about making the other person feel badly about himself and thus try harder to please (usually without the specific information needed to do so).

A good definition of *criticism* is that it is an opinion dressed as fact (or sometimes, particularly with children, as a rhetorical question). "Why can't you *ever* find pants and a shirt that match? Your younger sister does it just fine!" is criticism. "I don't think those pants match that shirt. Let's see if we can find an outfit we both like" contains an honest opinion and is feedback. Criticism often involves generalities ("why can't you *ever*") and comparison to others ("your sister does it just fine"). Feedback offers an indisputable fact ("your shoes have mud all over them") and is often accompanied by a directive ("please take them off before coming into the house").

Keeping these clear definitions in mind, make sure you use feedback instead of criticism with your child—and everyone else. Make a family rule that no one puts anyone down in the family, including adults and siblings. To a four-year-old, a five-year-old is an adult and always right, and anything said in your house or hearing will be seen as condoned by you. Ensure that consequences are enforced.

Teaching your children not to criticize others in the house, including you, can start as early as three. "I hate you!" is an honest expression of feeling (at the time). But "You're stupid!" should be countered with "We don't say that sort of thing in this family."

Gottman identifies "Four Horsemen of the Apocalypse" that damage family relationships. In addition to criticism, he cites defensiveness, contempt, and stonewalling. These, he says, are the most reliable predictors of divorce or of a long but miserable marriage or, we would add, a depressed child. But, as he says, you can learn to consistently "build in the antidotes."[10]

We believe that these are the best antidotes:

- Instead of criticism, give feedback or honest opinions.

- Instead of defensiveness, accept responsibility for a part of the problem.

- Instead of contempt, look sincerely at the other person's point of view.

- Instead of stonewalling, look for compromise. Make sure the other person sees that you're listening and let him know what you need to feel safe enough to move forward. Where compromise is not possible, honestly say so.

Tip: Beware of veiled criticism and sarcasm. Critical comments made in jest can be just as hurtful as outright criticism.

CURIOSITY AND INVOLVEMENT

Part of the mutual admiration system inherent in a culture of praise is showing curiosity about the interests, activities, and opinions of other family members.

Couples often tell us that they have "nothing in common." She will say: "He's only interested in sports [or the stock market or the newspaper]," and he will retort: "She's only interested in gossiping with friends and that New Age stuff." The subtext here is: "He/she isn't interested in me. I feel demeaned and criticized for being engaged in the things I enjoy." In the same way, a young child will say: "You never listen to me, ever!" or "You don't understand!"

If his opinions and interests are dismissed, your child will quickly learn that he himself doesn't matter—just as you will. Part of praise is taking the time to take an interest.

Donna and her husband, Charles, were both busy commercial artists living in Manhattan. Their five-year-old daughter, Daisy, had been diagnosed as depressed. She displayed a general lack of enthusiasm or interest, frequent bouts of temper, an inability to make friends, and generalized and unspecified aches and pains. She sat in Bob's office between her parents, her eyes fixed on her shoes.

"We don't know what to do with her," Donna began. "We can't get through to her." Charles nodded.

"Daisy," Bob said to the child. "Why do you think you're here?"

"Because I'm bad."

"You're not bad, honey," Charles said reassuringly. "You're just sad."

"I'm bad 'cause I'm sad!" The child was still looking at her shoes.

"I'd like to get to know you, would that be OK?" Bob asked.

" 'Suppose so."

"What games do you like?"

"Games are all stupid."

"All stupid? Who says that?"

"My dad, and my mom sometimes."

Donna and Charles were about to butt in, but Bob signaled them to be quiet.

"When do they say that?"

"They don't now, 'cause I don't play." She looked up for the first time.

"If you did play, what game would you choose?"

"Toads!"

"Can you show me the toad game?"

She looked at her mother, who gave a reluctant nod. The little girl got off the chair, gathered up some cushions from the spare chairs, and squatted on the floor. She started making Kermit-like noises, and each time she did, she threw a cushion.

"What are the cushions?" Bob asked her.

"Toads, of course!"

"And they make a noise when they jump?"

"Yes!" She smiled for the first time.

"Can I join in?"

"Can you be a toad?"

"Yes, but you'll have to make the noise."

For a few minutes, Bob hopped around the room every time Daisy made a frog noise. "What do you know about toads?" Bob asked her after a while.

"They're slimy and gooey, and they hop."

"I didn't know that," Bob said with interest. "I'll bet your mom could draw you a toad. Would you like that?" Daisy nodded. "And maybe your dad knows something about toads. Would it be OK if he told you some toad stories?"

The parents left the session with a "prescription" for lots of toad activities as well as instruction in other "depression-proofing" techniques. As her parents learned to take a genuine interest in what interested their child, Daisy's enthusiasm returned and she began to make friends (the toad game proved quite a hit with the preschool set). Her anger and mysterious pains also faded.

Remember that at the bedrock of every child's game is something that he's interested in, something important to him. Validating that enthusiasm is an integral part of a culture of praise.

10

STEP 7:
DEVELOP AND
NURTURE SHARED
VALUES AND BELIEFS

◉

Core values, shared beliefs, and rituals hold us together as a family, company, club, and nation. Common beliefs give us our sense of optimism, mutual values allow us to see each other as fundamentally "good" people, and rituals express these two aspects of our lives.

Yet these are the very attributes developed societies have lost. Largely as a result, many if not most families we come across seem to flounder through life with no solid core or fixed compass. Goaded on by insecurity and conflicting messages from a fractured society, they struggle to attain the outward symbols of success and acceptance: a better house or report card; the right school or job; the coolest Play Station; and the most up-to-date home theater system. Such families have nothing permanent to fall back on, nothing firm in their relationships or spiritual life to buffer them in times of stress. With no common ground in their relationships, stress more easily creates fractures that widen under pressure. We are still amazed at how few couples discuss early on their core values and beliefs in concrete terms, particularly regarding how they will chart their family life and raise their children.

FALSE VALUES

The values children learn very early shape their entire lives. If they believe that their personal worth lies in who they are rather than what they achieve and that relationships and spirituality are more important than having the biggest yard or the coolest toys, they are well on the path to shaping their lives on a solid basis that provides optimism and emotional health.

Researchers Suniya S. Luthar, Ph.D., and Bronwyn E. Becker of Columbia University found in a 2002 study that achievement pressures begin very early in a child's life and ultimately lead, in a large proportion of their study subjects, to early drug use, alcoholism, and depression.

These achievement pressures, they noted, include messages about parental values rooted in materialism as well as "maladaptive perfectionism"—not merely striving for high and realistic goals, but developing an "excessive investment in accomplishments and need to avoid failure."

"In upwardly mobile suburban communities," they wrote, "there is often a ubiquitous emphasis on ensuring that children secure admission to stellar colleges. As a result, many youngsters feel highly driven to excel not only at academics but also at multiple extracurricular activities."[1] Indeed, parents often complain to us that their kid "flunked kindergarten" and thus, they believe, endangered his chances of entry into a good college.

According to Peggy Papp, director of the Depression Project at the Ackerman Institute for Family Therapy in New York, these unstated materialistic and achievement-oriented values are prevalent in our culture and lead to parents prioritizing work ahead of their children or creating unrealistic and dysfunctional expectations—all of which can lead to depression.

Just as damaging as false values is incongruity between what parents say and what they do. A few years ago the magazine *National Demographics* asked a large number of executives in a diverse range of industries to list their core values. At the top of the list were "home and family," yet their actions showed that they preferred to stay at their workplace, even when taking more time to be with their families involved no financial sacrifice. Such mixed messages make even a very young child feel pessimistic and distrustful of adults.

TEACHING POSITIVE VALUES

To help ensure a child's optimism and freedom from depression, a family's values must:

- Be expressed concretely and openly acknowledged

- Involve altruism and doing good for others (We are an altruistic species, and research shows that people feel happier, are healthier mentally and physically, and live longer if they help others.[2])

- Show up as actions by adults in the family (There's no point in subscribing to a set of values that you ignore in practice—and it's bad for the kids.)

- Allow family members to feel good about themselves (Values must not provoke excessive feelings of guilt. For example, the belief that people are only worthwhile for what they achieve or own leads to a sense of inadequacy. Beliefs that cause shame about the body or natural functions obviously cause guilt, as do values or beliefs that are impossible to live up to given the family's circumstances or environment.)

- Be values that you would like your family to be remembered as having

- Acknowledge the legitimate rights of others, including those of other races, beliefs, income, age, appearance, beliefs, and education (If any person can be seen as unimportant or even persecuted for these reasons, no one can feel really secure, and it will be hard to teach children a sense of "fairness" that has any meaning.)

A set of values that have these qualities can be a very powerful cohesive force within the family and add to the mental health of its members. Demitri and Janice Papolos, in their book *The Bipolar Child*, illustrate how one community—the Amish—that adheres to a set of values along these lines can have children who are protected against a most insidious form of depressive illness, bipolar disorder. They contend that "[t]he regularity and simplicity of the Amish lifestyle, characterized by consistent social values, a philosophy of nonviolence, strong family and community kinship structures . . . may modify many behaviors that could reach their extreme pitch in families that do not have such defined social and religious values and cannot provide such consistent boundaries."[3]

Tip: Take the opportunity to discuss values after watching a TV show or reading a book. Ask your children, for example, what makes a character a good guy or a bad guy.

FAMILY MISSION STATEMENT

You can help your family develop a core of shared values and give your children a healthy sense of life purpose by jointly producing what Stephen Covey, in his book *The 7 Habits of Highly Effective People*, calls a Family Mission Statement. "By writing a Family Mission Statement you give expression to [the family's] true foundation. This mission statement becomes its constitution, the standard, the criterion for evaluation and decision-making. It gives continuity and unity to the family as well as direction. When individual values are harmonized with those of the family, members work together for common purposes that are deeply felt," says Covey.[4]

So what's the how-to of a Family Mission Statement? By now you'll probably agree that the first and most obvious place to start is at a Family Powwow. At this powwow, all members over the age of three should be encouraged to state what their values are. Your four-year-old is not your arbiter of values, nor does she understand such concepts, but being invited helps teach her that her views, thoughts, and ideas matter. You can engage her in the process by explaining family values in her terms; for example, illustrate the importance of ecological conservation by pointing out her favorite trees or flowers in your yard or nearby park and say it's about making sure no one takes them away or hurts them.

Write down all the agreed values. Remember that the process is as important as the finished document. By getting input from all the family members, debating, discussing, and revising to accommodate other people's ideas, everyone practices forming their own values and finding common ground with others. You can write each member's contribution on a blackboard or poster-size butcher paper with the name of the contributor at the bottom of the page. The kids might enjoy decorating the pages, being careful not to draw over the writing. Leave the writing on the blackboard for a while, or put the paper up on the walls (perhaps in the family room or den) to remind everyone of what you stand for as a family.

Implementing Your Vision

There are two parts to a Family Mission Statement: vision and practice. The series of value statements we've just discussed form the basis for the vision, the ultimate purposes for which the family exists. Once you reach agreement and acceptance of the vision, you then move on to the practice, stating the concrete actions that you, as a family, will take to implement the vision.

For example, one of your vision statements might be: "We as a family believe in the value of lifelong education." (Note that this does not just say "education," because otherwise the kids might think this is something of a trick aimed at them. Adding *lifelong* assumes that the parents believe in education for themselves as well.)

Under practice you might write (on a notepad, blackboard, or your butcher paper):

- We will cooperate with the teachers at school (e.g., kids will do as the teachers say and parents will meet with teachers regularly).

- We will join and support the PTA.

- We will contribute 1 percent of our income to educational charities.

- We will discuss our studies together and help each other understand what we are learning.

Keep a final record of your Family Mission Statement. Of course, it can be revised at a later time, and it should evolve as your family members do.

VALUES FOR HAPPINESS

Can our values make us happy? Research shows that a strong set of *the right kind of values*, such as self-worth, good relationships, and a connection to nature, does indeed lead to happiness.[5]

Professor Stephen Reiss of Ohio State University says that there are two types of happiness: feel-good happiness and value happiness. "Feel-good happiness is sensation-based pleasure. When we joke around or have sex, we experience feel-good happiness. Since feel-good happiness is ruled by the law of diminishing returns, the kicks get harder to come by. This type of happiness rarely lasts longer than a few hours at a time. Value-based happiness is a sense that our lives have meaning and fulfill some larger purpose. It represents a spiritual source of satisfaction, stemming from our deeper purpose and values."[6]

Value happiness has strong links to self-esteem. Research by Robert Atkins, a psychology professor at Ohio State, has shown that chronic self-doubters are most likely to be materialistic and to agree with statements such as "I like to own things that impress people" and "The things I own say a lot about how well I'm doing in life."[7]

In order to teach your children how to find a deeper source of satisfaction than materialism, try the following:

- Do lots of fun, nature-related activities as a family and with friends, such as walking in a national park, playing at the beach, picking berries or edible herbs, and tending a garden or even houseplants.

- Make a family project of fixing or building things rather than always buying new ones.

- Read (and teach your child to read) stories that reinforce your family values, including perhaps classics such as the *Chronicles of Narnia* by C. S. Lewis, *Horton Hears a Who* by Dr. Seuss, *Charlotte's Web* by E. B. White, and *Winnie the Pooh* by A. A. Milne.

- Be playful with each other as well as the kids.

- Take time for games and storytelling, which demonstrate that just being together is a good time.

SPIRITUALITY:
THE ULTIMATE ANTIDEPRESSANT

Numerous recent studies, many from Duke University Medical Center under the aegis of Professor Harold Koenig, have shown that spirituality, in all its manifestations, is perhaps the most powerful antidepressant.[8] Without spiritual values, our lives are empty; without a belief system, we are lost; without a meaningful sense of connection to the world around us, we are isolated.

The need for a belief in something greater than ourselves that in some way cares for us and looks after us is embedded in our genes and wired into our brain. Scientists even believe they have found the system of neural connections, dubbed the "God module," that specializes in belief—and not surprisingly, it's also linked to our sense of optimism.[9]

Prominent Norwegian biologist Bjørn Grinde, an admitted atheist, notes that as science lessens the impact of religion, society becomes sadder and more pessimistic. He writes that the need for religious belief is embedded in our genes and that it performs the useful survival functions of giving people hope, guiding them toward more altruistic behavior, and strengthening group cohesion.[10]

Another part of the brain—which is called the posterior superior parietal lobe (PSPL) and is involved in spatial awareness—plays a vital role in meditation and prayer. Under normal circumstances, this area is a hive of activity, keeping you constantly aware of where your body ends and where you are in relation to things around you.

However, during intense prayer or meditation the PSPL becomes a quiet oasis of inactivity. Professor Andrew Newburg of Pennsylvania University, who discovered the area, says that when activated it "creates a blurring of the self-other relationship. If meditators go far enough they have a complete dissolving of the self, a sense of union, a sense of infinite spacelessness" and contact with the divine.[11] We are also able to access this surrender of the self when we connect deeply with nature or when we have an overwhelming religious experience.

> **Tip:** Meditating just fifteen minutes twice a day not only keeps you healthy but boosts your energy and parenting patience. Make sure you keep it up because the full benefits really kick in after eight months.[12]

Spirituality in Practice

Spiritual values and activities are a means of strengthening and accessing inner peace as parents, providing grounding in optimism for you and your child, and reinforcing family togetherness. Under the practice section of your Family Mission Statement, you might therefore regularly include some of the following:

- Meditation (Those under age six can be invited if they are very, very quiet, later joining in more fully.)

- Prayer (Everyone can join in mealtime prayers.)

- Family rituals and ceremonies

- Attendance at places of worship

- Nature walks in which you point out the wonder and beauty of all living things

- Activities in support of ecological causes

- Volunteering with humane societies and talking about the value of all forms of life

- Pet ownership (Dogs, cats, horses, and ferrets form relationships with us that enable us to get out of ourselves and care for another creature.)

- Study of religion and/or spirituality

- Yoga or our own Repatterning Movements[13] (Your kids will enjoy showing off their amazing flexibility!)

- Music you can lose yourself in and/or the kids can dance (or jiggle) to

We are sometimes asked: "Should we inculcate our children in a certain religious or spiritual belief or wait until they are mature enough to choose their own?" Our answer is definitely to offer your children a vibrant belief system and make the accompanying rituals a strong part of family life. One of New York's top corporate lawyers was brought up as a churchgoer but stopped going to services when he left home. Because his wife felt strongly about bringing the children up in their faith, he agreed and became involved in the local church, making sure the children attended Sunday school and other church functions. "It's part of what bonds us now as a family," he says. "But my faith gives me a sense of inner strength and solace as well."

It's important for you and your partner to demonstrate what is important to you by your actions and not just by your words. For instance, your actions should show that you *value* a deep connection to other people based on the mutual satisfaction of needs, that you *value* spirituality, that you *value* the sanctity of all living things, that you *value* nature for herself and not just as a tourist attraction. By making your values, beliefs, and rituals the heart of your family life, you can provide your children with ways of being happy that don't depend on their having the latest clothes, video games, or gadgets. Finding joy in activities related to these values offers all members lifelong resilience and protects them from the lure of consumerism, premature or inappropriate sex, and substance abuse—all of which lead directly to pessimism and depression.

PART III

APPLYING OPTIMISTIC PARENTING STRATEGIES TO COMMON CHALLENGES

11

PREVENTING THE
CONSEQUENCES OF
PARENTAL DEPRESSION

⊙

Perhaps the most important action you can take to address or prevent your child's depression is to make sure you attend to any depression of your own (or your partner's).

More than 20 percent of parents of young children suffer from a mood disorder such as depression, anxiety, or posttraumatic stress disorder (PTSD). Postnatal depression affects 15 percent of mothers and is linked to isolation[1] and stress, as well as hormonal imbalances. Research shows that children of depressed parents are at high risk for depression themselves, as well as for substance abuse and other antisocial behaviors. Depressed mothers have difficulty bonding with their infants and thus may be less sensitive to the baby's needs, less emotionally involved, and less consistent in their responses to his behavior. As a result, these babies often appear more unhappy and isolated than others. They may seem listless and can be difficult to comfort, feed, and put to sleep. As toddlers, these children are very often hard to handle—defiant, negative, and rejecting of parental authority. Unfortunately, this reinforces the depressed parent's sense of failure. Because nothing seems to work, the parent's actions are likely to remain inconsistent.

Moreover, studies show that the vast majority of parents blame their own low feelings on their "difficult" children. Have you ever seen those stickers that say something like: "I'm crazy, and I inherited it from my children"? These are amusing, but they reveal a deep-seated belief. "Damian is so difficult, I just can't cope anymore, and my physician has prescribed antidepressants," one mother of a recalcitrant four-year-old lamented to us. When we talked more, she realized that she had been depressed during her pregnancy and perhaps even earlier, when she felt isolated and ignored by her husband. The stress she attributed to Damian had in fact started long before his birth and contributed to his problems.

"Though the parents often feel that the child's behavior is the source of their distress, it usually makes more sense to hypothesize that the child is reacting to the parent's depression,"[2] says author and psychologist Richard O'Connor. "When the depressed parent isn't able to get help . . . the outlook isn't good for the child. He or she grows up with dangerous and destructive ideas about the self—that he's unlovable, uncontrollable, and a general nuisance. He doesn't know how to get attention from adults in positive ways, so gets labeled a 'troublemaker.' He doesn't know how to soothe himself, so is at risk for substance abuse. He doesn't know he's a worthwhile human being, so is at risk for depression. He hasn't learned how to control his own behavior, so he can't fit into school or work."[3]

Depressed and addicted parents share the same sorts of parenting problems, and their children display the same types of "difficult" or antisocial patterns of behavior.[4] According to Catherine Stanger, professor at the University of Vermont, 20 percent of people in treatment for drug dependence are parents of young children. What's lacking in the household of both depressed and addicted parents are consistency and empathy. A toddler's "bad" behavior is often a cry for help, an attempt to get his parents to establish consistent rules or even to notice him in some meaningful way.

DEALING WITH YOUR DEPRESSION

Becoming an empathic and consistent parent requires you to address your own problems. The following strategies will help if you suffer depression, anxiety, or addiction or are having difficulty coping.

1. Admit your problem and seek help from your partner, friends, and professionals.

2. Monitor your behavior.

3. Build your own self-esteem and competence.

4. Express appropriate optimism.

ADMIT YOUR PROBLEM AND SEEK HELP

If you are depressed, the first step to healing the disorder, or at least making sure that it impacts as little as possible on your family, is to acknowledge you have a problem and seek help. Without help for the parent, there can be no hope for the child. Yet sometimes this is the hardest step to take. Despite all the information now available about depression as an illness, not a weakness, we may still feel ashamed that we can't somehow "pull ourselves up by the bootstraps." We feel even more guilty when we consider the impact our mood is having on our child, and our guilt may paralyze us.

In order to overcome our guilt and regain control over our lives, it's important to remember that we are not our depression and that it is not our fault. Depression is largely a childhood legacy that we do not choose but that we can overcome. It is related to childhood trauma and feeds on our shame and secrecy—traits we may have learned very young.

Secrets are at the core of many troubled nuclear families—perhaps of the institution itself. The prominent British anthropologist Edmund Leach famously said of the modern overstressed family: "Far from being the basis of the good society, the family, with its narrow privacy and tawdry secrets, is the source of all our discontents."[5] In Stone Age times, before people began living in villages, towns, and cities, it was impossible to keep secrets because of the communal way people lived. There are no separate rooms in a cave! If there was a problem in a particular unit of the band, everybody knew about it and help would be forthcoming.[6]

In our society, many if not most families have secrets: they can include parental fighting, addiction, poverty (or just not having as much as the neighbors), job loss, emotional illness, or abuse. Even toddlers learn early to keep quiet about certain things. In fact, research has shown that younger children are more likely to keep secrets than older ones.[7] Disclosing family secrets makes children feel shame and great anxiety and this, as research by Barry Farber of Columbia University has shown, can continue into adulthood and disrupt relationships.[8] A child who feels that he has to keep secrets will avoid making friendships and remain secretive throughout life.

Help from Your Partner or Best Friend

If you find it difficult to talk about your problems, whether because of a family history of secretiveness or simply fear no one will understand, start by thinking of one person you might trust with your confidence. Hopefully, this would be your partner, but it could also be a trusted friend. The guidelines below may help you begin. (Note: Because we use "him" and "her" in alternating chapters, we sometimes refer in these guidelines to the partner or friend giving help as "him." Obviously, however, the depressed person is just as likely to be male and the other female.)

• Ask yourself, what would you need this person to do or not to do in order for you to feel safe in telling him of your depression or related problems? Examples might be: "I need you to keep what I'm about to tell you confidential. Can you agree?" Or, "I need you not to tell me just to 'snap out of it' if I tell you how I feel."

• Think also of what you need this person to do to help you overcome the problem, and write down a concrete and action-oriented Needs List. It's not just that you want him to feel compassion or understand where you're coming from, but also to take actions that will convince you that he does. Examples of needs around this issue are: "I need you to ask me what's wrong when you see me looking sad." "I need you to set aside fifteen minutes each day to talk to me about what I'm feeling or what's gone on during the day." "I need you to encourage me to see my friends and suggest I call them if I haven't." "I need you to praise me for how I'm bringing up the children."

• Let this person know in advance that you have something important to discuss, and set aside a generous amount of time when the children are in bed or won't interrupt. (If you can't find the time, this is part of the problem, and you both need to work out ways to address it.)

• At the meeting, tell this person what you need him to do in order for you to feel comfortable confiding in him and, if he agrees, continue, taking as much time as you need.

• Begin with how your problem is affecting your life right now. For example, you might start by saying: "You may have noticed that I have been tired and irritable lately, and I've been short with both you and Yolanda, well. . . ."

• When you've finished, allow your partner or friend to ask questions and express his feelings. If he wasn't aware of your depression (or addiction, or perhaps a trauma from childhood that's affecting you now), he may well berate himself for not seeing it. Allow him to feel that (you can't rescue him from his feelings), but acknowledge that you've been good at keeping the secret.

• Be very clear what you need him to do to help you overcome the problem. If he can't agree to the needs now, set a time for another discussion. Be sure to ask him to tell you his needs of you if he hasn't already done so—if you don't know how (or if) you're meeting his needs, you don't have the emotional security that's vital to overcome depression.

• End the discussion with a promise that there will be no more secrets in the future and get him to agree to that as well.

Help from Friends and Coworkers

Next, enlist help from your other friends and colleagues. The Beatles song "I Get by with a Little Help from My Friends" almost sums up human beings. Our genes provide us with the capacity to make friends so that they can help us in difficult times.[9] Admitting your depression may be challenging at first, but it is ultimately liberating. If you can't open up to your friends, ask yourself whether it's because you find it difficult to talk about personal things or whether you've been put off by their reactions in the past. If it's the latter, you may be hanging out with the wrong crowd!

Opening up to work colleagues who aren't close friends can be even more daunting, and you may need to really think about whom you can trust and what the repercussions might be. However, most enlightened firms now recognize that depression is a prevalent condition affecting 30 percent of corporate employees, not a personal failing. A good manager or professional colleague would use the information to work out ways to give you the assistance you need to overcome or manage the problem. If your depression is serious, it may well affect your work performance, and it's better that those you work with know the real reason your work may be suffering.

You enlist the support of a good, trustworthy friend or work colleague in much the same way you do your partner, although you may not talk about the same issues or do so in the same depth. Work out a preliminary Needs List; put quality time aside for the conversation; insist your friend or colleague listen without making judgments; and tell him your needs, either in the form of a formal Needs List or a few at a time. If he really is a good friend, altruism will do the rest. You may even find that this person has secrets to share with you. Well and good, but make sure your friend or coworker understands that this is your time and that you can be there for him more fully as you get stronger.

Tip: Once you've told a few people close to you about your depression, you can lead up gradually to telling others. "I feel flat (or 'low') today. Does that ever happen to you?" is a good way to test the waters with people you aren't sure about. If they respond with empathy, it's a good indication that you may be able to disclose more either then or later.

Professional Help

Your partner and friends are vital, but if you have severe, ongoing depression, you will probably find it helpful to speak to someone who fully understands the problem and won't be personally affected by what you say. It's important to make sure you find the right therapist for you, which is not always easy, given that there are many different types of therapists and many approaches. There are some important criteria to keep in mind when choosing a therapist.

• You should feel very comfortable talking to the therapist. Don't be afraid to speak to a number of practitioners before choosing. Writing a Needs List for a practitioner beforehand will help keep the initial consultation focused on your concerns and determine if the person is willing to meaningfully address them.

• The therapist you select should have the training and experience to understand your difficulty. If you are considering medication, a consultation with a psychiatrist may be useful. However, a psychiatrist is often not trained in psychotherapy and is sometimes hampered by a medical model that relies primarily on medication. Psychologists have the most academic training after psychiatrists, followed by psychotherapists, who may have a degree in psychology or social work, and counselors, who tend to specialize in particular fields such as alcoholism, family therapy, or education. Good sources for referrals include the American Psychological Association (apa.org), the Association for Humanistic Psychologists (ahpweb.org), and the American Counseling Association (counseling.org). A number of professionals have studied the Fortinberry-Murray Method and Uplift principles (uplift program.com).

• The therapist should have the skill to help you link past influences to present patterns and take actions to change. Just having you "reframe" your experience positively or substitute "positive" for "negative" thoughts doesn't heal depression in the long term. In fact, new research shows that these suppressed thoughts may come back more strongly than ever when control inevitably falters.[10]

• The therapist should be willing to work with approaches you feel are helping you. If that includes the Uplift approach, ask if the practitioner would support you in defeating the "inner saboteur" and doing needs work.

• The costs of the therapist's services should fit your budget. Don't be shy about asking about costs and whether sessions are covered by your health plan. Of course, the overall cost will be determined by how long you work together. Taking the action steps listed in *Creating Optimism: A Proven Seven-Step Program for Overcoming Depression* as well as this book will enormously speed up your recovery.

You can experience an intensive immersion in our powerful seven-step program for overcoming depression in our internationally acclaimed Uplift Program, which is sponsored by a number of major international organizations, including the University of South Florida. Often we teach these courses ourselves.

Talking to Your Child

Getting appropriate help prevents an unfortunate tendency some parents have to burden their children with emotional problems they can't understand or help—nor is it their job. But that doesn't mean you should—or indeed can—keep problems such as depression, severe anxiety, or addiction a secret. Children, even very young ones, will assume your unhappiness or erratic moods and behavior are somehow their fault and in many cases spend the rest of their lives trying to rescue you (and, later, surrogates) and punish themselves for failing.

Never, ever blame your mood on something your child did or failed to do. You can say that specific actions hurt you or make you sad: "It hurts Mommy when you hit me (or call me bad names, or tear up my papers, etc.)." But avoid linking your mood to your child's behavior in general. "No wonder Mommy is in a bad mood when you kids fight all the time." It's very harmful, and it's simply not true. Your child doesn't cause your depression.

You and your partner should explain that sometimes Mommy or Daddy is upset or even grumpy, but that doesn't mean the child has done anything wrong. In fact, since depression stems from your own childhood, it's a good idea to say that often what's really making you feel these things happened a long, long time ago, before your child was born. Repeat this frequently, particularly when you are in a difficult mood. But say that Daddy (or Mommy) and lots of other people are helping and that you will feel better soon. Your child will idealize and later emulate sharing secrets and drawing on others' support and, hopefully, see the productive results.

You can talk to older children more fully about your problem, where it came from and what triggers it. Make sure they know that you are taking steps to manage it and the job does not fall on them.

> **Tip:** Speak to your child often about feelings—yours and his—and explain that even the sad ones will pass. Then hearing about your sad or depressed feelings won't be as upsetting.

MONITOR YOUR BEHAVIOR

To slightly misquote a well-known saying attributed to Thomas Jefferson: "The price of liberty from depression is eternal vigilance." Monitoring your behavior toward those around you, especially your child, is vital. Sometimes you can slip into depressive behaviors well before you feel depressed. Signs to watch for are:

- Anger and irritability, especially at those close to you

- Instances of being critical or argumentative

- Withdrawal—canceling dates and appointments, not picking up the telephone or returning calls, answering questions in monosyllables

- Excessive or inadequate sleep

- Lack of interest in what you used to enjoy or lack of pleasure in general

These behaviors and feelings can be signs like the canary in the mine. Immediately tell your partner, friends, mental health professional, and child, if he is older than three, that you feel you might be relapsing. This will give them the chance to make allowances and to take actions to help you. The sooner you galvanize your support network into action, the shorter the depressive episode will last and the smallest amount of damage will be done to your child.

In the meantime, try to pause before making angry, critical, or upsetting remarks, especially to your child. Counting to ten really does help, especially when you use the time to remind yourself that the strength of your anger comes from the past. Your young child isn't out to hurt you, so perhaps he reminds your unconscious of an early relationship that caused you pain. If you feel overwhelmed by negative emotions, give yourself a "time-out." Call your partner, friend, practitioner, or even, if you feel you might lose control and hurt yourself or your child, a help line. If your child is safe on his own for a bit, take a shower or meditate. If not, ask a neighbor or friend to come over and give you a break while you take a walk or do anything else that you find calming.

Tip: Often we don't notice our depressive symptoms. Ask other people you trust to honestly—and gently—tell you when they notice you becoming upset, angry, critical, or withdrawn.

BUILD YOUR SELF-ESTEEM

Lack of true self-esteem and a sense of competence are underlying causes of depression, and a threat to these can trigger a depressive episode. Your infant's or toddler's sense of self-worth will very largely be a reflection of yours, so it's doubly important to attend to it.

As much as we might like to see ourselves as emotionally self-sufficient, our self-worth depends largely on the praise we receive and the regard others show us. Therefore, your Needs List should clearly express how you would like people to praise you and give you functional importance in all areas of your life. Also, be very careful to avoid not only criticism from others, but self-put-downs, such as "stupid me" or "this may sound silly, but. . . ." (You wouldn't want your child to say these things about himself, would you? So don't model self-denigration!)

Not surprisingly, your values play an important role in authentic self-esteem. Recent research shows that how you go about boosting your sense of self-worth and what you attach that self-worth to are actually more important than whether your self-esteem is high or low. In 2004 Jennifer Crocker and Laura Park of the University of Michigan discovered that many people invested their self-esteem in superficial areas (such as what they earn, own, or drive) that they then defended "in ways that undermine learning; relatedness; autonomy and self-regulation; and over time, mental and physical health. The short-term emotional benefits of pursuing self-esteem are often outweighed by long-term costs."[11]

If, on the other hand, your self-esteem is directed toward what Crocker and Park call "adaptive ends" (psychologically worthwhile goals), then "it can be instrumental in promoting long-term outcomes that are of value to both individuals and society."[12]

In building adaptive self-esteem for yourself and your children, you may find it helpful to revisit the Family Mission Statement (see Chapter 10) and, with the help of your partner, friends, and, perhaps, therapist, strive to build your self-esteem around your true values and goals. In addition:

- Insist that people praise you often and appropriately and never criticize.

- Make sure your needs are met in all areas of your life.

- Pursue passions and activities you enjoy the process of.

- Be open about any difficulties you have around job performance, from dyslexia to depression, and allow people to help you be effective at what you do.

EXPRESS APPROPRIATE OPTIMISM

Depression causes people to be negative and pessimistic, and this outlook may be one of the ways you pass on depression to your child. Both optimism and pessimism are largely learned. If you're constantly saying "that won't work" or "it's not good enough," whether you are speaking of yourself or your child, he will come to believe that things won't ever turn out right, including himself. This, of course, becomes a self-fulfilling prophecy.

Real, appropriate optimism is not a Pollyanna-like belief that everything that happens is always for the best or mouthing positive platitudes; it's taking a balanced view. Make sure that your expectations of any outcomes are reasonable, so that you set yourself up for success rather than failure.

Here are some suggestions for engendering appropriate optimism:

- Catch yourself before making a knee-jerk negative comment, and if you do, quickly add a more positive one, for example "but even if it does rain tomorrow, it may well stop long enough for us to go for a walk."

- Surround yourself, as much as possible, with optimistic people. Your brain will learn from their outlook.

- Ask people around you to remind you when things are going well and to question, where appropriate and without judgment, your negative outlook.

- Test your beliefs about negative outcomes against those of people you respect but whom you know have a balanced outlook.

- Before you undertake any project, work out with your partner, colleagues, or friends what would be a reasonable outcome and set your sights on that.

Even if it takes a while to turn your pessimism into optimism, if your child sees that you are challenging your own pessimistic outlook, he will be far more likely to develop a more balanced view. In the same way, as you continue to work in these ways to overcome your depression, he will learn that problems can often be overcome with determination—and a little help from your friends.

12

MORE OPTIMISTIC
PARENTING SKILLS

◉

Contrary to popular—and some professional—beliefs, pessimistic thoughts don't *cause* depression but *result* from the same factors that underlie the disorder: childhood stress and trauma. In fact, depression and pessimism are neurologically similar,[1] and our entire seven-step program addresses both. But fostering a positive mind-set in your child will certainly help ward off depression, and this chapter presents some powerful additional optimistic parenting skills.

Given reasonable circumstances, children up to about age seven are wildly optimistic, according to Kristi L. Lockhart of Yale University. Her study shows that kindergarteners and first graders believe that people are capable of undergoing dramatic transformations, trading negative traits for positive ones; that the least intelligent person could become the smartest and the meanest the nicest; and even that it's possible to grow back a missing finger. This innate optimism emboldens children to tackle new challenges, learn new skills, risk new relationships, and persevere.

Between ages seven and ten, a more balanced but still positive outlook is meant to take over, although the child's genes will play a role in determining whether she is more drawn to risk or caution.[2] Both these points of view are necessary for a hunter-gatherer band, although without a prevailing optimism our species would go the way of the dodo.

Part of the job of a family is to make sure that this natural optimism does not give way to what psychology professor Martin Seligman of Pennsylvania University calls "learned helplessness," a style of pessimistic thought resulting from constant disappointments and frustrations that he blames for the depression epidemic.[3]

THE FIVE PRINCIPLES OF HAPPY PARENTING

There are five keys to an optimistic outlook, and they are best learned early. These "HAPPY" principles involve promoting a sense of mastery and competence by taking on realistic challenges, succeeding, and persevering. The resulting experiences of success foster both an expectation that things will go well and resilience in the face of discouragement. In order to instill these principles in your child, encourage her to:

Have a go.
Accept both success and failure.
Practice.
Plan for the best outcome.
Yes! Make optimism and an upbeat confidence a lifelong habit.

ENCOURAGE "HAVING A GO"

Australians, whose origins as convicts in a harsh environment have made them very plucky, use the phrase "have a go" a lot, and it means to take a chance, to try. In order to encourage your child to get into the habit of "having a go," provide the right mixture of support and challenges right from the start. Children are natural explorers, and giving them a rich environment full of colors, movement, textures, and a variety of surfaces helps them begin the exciting sensory and kinesthetic process of mastering their world. You provide the safety and encouragement, showing her how pleased you are with every attempt at something new and giving a hand when she needs it.

An infant learns through games, such as peek-a-boo, and tracking your face or objects with her eyes and ears. As she gets older, play games that encourage her to use new words or clamber over awkward objects to reach you or her favorite toy. At four or five, she can accept even greater challenges, for example, reading or finding her way home (with you) from places that are increasingly distant. Remember that your encouragement, your praise, is what she wants even more than the "goal" she's striving for.

Tip: It's important to break games into manageable pieces so that she can succeed. Never let her know you are disappointed if she fails, or she may simply give up trying.

ACCEPTING SUCCESS AND FAILURE

A stanza in Rudyard Kipling's poem "If" says it all about balanced optimism:

If you can meet with Triumph and Disaster
And treat those two imposters just the same.

While you must do all you can to ensure that your child experiences triumphs as she gains mastery over her world, also teach her that no one succeeds all the time. Even Superman had kryptonite to deal with! Optimism means that your child can accept doing a particular task poorly and not believe that her efforts will always turn out badly. More than that, she can fail and still keep her sense of self, still be a worthwhile person.

Problems often occur when parents unconsciously attach their own self-esteem to their child's achievements. If you find yourself unhappy about your child's accomplishment (or lack of it), ask yourself how that feeling might tie into your own self-worth and your parents' reactions to you when you were a child.

How you "frame"—or put into context—the outcome of a particular event for your child will largely determine her reaction and teach her how to interpret such situations in the future. Praising her for trying and for how she did something rather than just the outcome will help maintain her confidence and perseverance. For example, if your child loses a swimming race, validate her feelings if she's sad or frustrated, but add something like: "I think you did great. You didn't give up, and you moved your arms just like you practiced in swim class."

Being able to accept a particular failure as part of the process of life rather than a disaster means not "catastrophizing" setbacks. Says Seligman, "Failure . . . may deflate self-esteem for a while, but it is the interpretation your child makes of the failure that can be more harmful."[4]

For example, if your child construes a problem with reading one sentence as "I'll *never* learn to read" or friends playing together without including her as "*No one* likes me," she will feel badly both about herself and life in general. You can help by pointing out that these negative events are not permanent or all-pervasive, but temporary and specific. Frame her experiences in a more positive light, by saying such things as "I know it's frustrating, but that was a really difficult sentence, and you read all the others!" Or, "Just because they didn't invite you this time doesn't mean that everyone doesn't like you. Maybe they didn't even see you." Just be sure to empathize with her feelings, whatever they are, and tell the truth as you see it, or if you are giving an opinion, say so.

Words like *always* and *never* are indications of what Seligman calls a "permanent pessimistic style." He says, "People who give up easily believe that the causes of the bad events that happen to them are permanent; the bad events will persist, will always be there to affect their lives. People who resist helplessness believe the causes of bad events are temporary."[5]

Children—and many adults—need to learn that the most important constants in life are close relationships, which provide the ultimate safety, security, and capacity for happiness.

All too often, adults become mesmerized by end goals and lose the ability to enjoy the process. Yet most of our life is spent in process—studying for a degree, exercising to get or stay in shape, traveling toward the destination. In fact, studies show that big events like a promotion or a new house don't affect our overall mood as much as our everyday experiences. Young children have the gift of focusing intently on the present without worrying about the outcome. Although you may need to instill a bit of realism (we'll be talking about delayed gratification in a moment), emphasize the pleasure of process. Model this approach by organizing your life as much as possible around what you enjoy the process of doing rather than what you feel you "should" do or what you believe will lead to a certain goal. Life's journey is almost all process, and most triumphs and disasters are but punctuation along the way.

> **Tip:** Make a note of all the times you say "always" or "never" in one day—and then think about the message you're passing on!

PRACTICE AND PERSEVERANCE

Encouraging children to practice skills and persevere can further enhance their sense of mastery and competence and create what psychologists Robert Brooks and Sam Goldstein call "islands of competence." "These," they write in *Raising Resilient Children*, "are activities that children do well, enjoy doing, receive positive regard for doing, and, most important, recognize as personal strengths."[6]

Even if at first children with very low confidence seem to disregard positive comments, resulting in parents' becoming frustrated and reducing positive feedback, it's important to hang in with praise. "True self-worth, hope, and resilience are based on a child's experiencing success in areas of their lives that they and others deem to be important," say Brooks and Goldstein. "This requires parents to identify and reinforce a child's islands of competence. . . . When children discover their strengths, they are more willing to confront even those areas that have proved to be problematic."[7]

For a small child, walking is a major accomplishment, one she's wired to achieve. Give her the means—objects to balance against, praise when she takes a step, a hand to grasp if she reaches out to you—and she will brilliantly activate this innate ability. Practicing her walking skills involves falling and getting up again. If you show impatience, rush her, or try to always hold her hands so she can't fall, she won't gain the confidence or sense of mastery. (She may also develop learning difficulties later on.) She won't discover how to learn skills through experimenting or when to ask for appropriate help. She'll learn that if things don't go well at first to give up and let someone else rescue her or solve the problem—in other words, she'll learn to be helpless.

Remember that all children have their own pace and ways of doing things. Your child will develop islands of competence around activities that excite her enthusiasm and curiosity, not necessarily yours! Be careful not to impose your interests and timing on her. The idea is not to raise a carbon copy of you or a precocious kid, but an optimistic, resilient, and ultimately autonomous human being.

Tip: Allowing your child to watch you practice and persevere at activities you enjoy will teach her to do the same.

PLANNING FOR THE BEST OUTCOME

The choice between taking an immediate reward now or waiting for a larger one later sets up a conflict in our brains between the emotional center—which is impulsive and will opt for the immediate return—and the more rational central cortex, which can plan and accept a delayed prize.[8]

Research has shown that children who are able to accept delayed rewards when they are very young tend to do better in school, their careers, and life in general. They are also more optimistic. Studies by Angela Prencipe and Philip David Zelazo of the University of Toronto have shown that two-year-olds choose smaller, but immediate, rewards over larger, but delayed, ones. Their cortex hasn't grown sufficiently to allow for reason and planning. By the time they reach four, they are able to apply more reason to the situation and accept a deferred reward. As Prencipe and Zelazo write, ". . . four-year-olds are better able to represent multiple aspects of a problem, formulate a plan, keep the plan in mind, and act on it deliberately."[9]

Children with attention deficit problems such as ADHD find planning very difficult. Insecure attachment, which creates the fear that mother may leave and must be clung to, may also inhibit the ability to accept deferred reward.

The best ways of training children age four and older how to plan for the future are to encourage them to think the situation over and show how you opt for future rewards that add real value to your life rather than immediate gratification. For example, explain to them that you aren't eating sour cream with your potato because, although it tastes good now, your body might feel bad later. And although you want a house with a bigger lawn to play on, you are waiting until there's more money in the bank so you can buy just the right home later and not have to worry. Spelling out the virtues of planning or waiting will get nowhere if you don't plan and you don't wait.

Obviously, ensuring that children feel secure in their relationships is also vital, as is encouraging them to expect good outcomes. Being realistically optimistic means knowing that often, perhaps even in the majority of instances, the things that you really want and that are worth planning for will happen. It's important that a child's natural joy in being included in the planning process is encouraged rather than seen as a nuisance. Involve children in planning for fun things—a visit to the beach, getting a puppy, an outing to the zoo, or a visit by a friend or relative.

To help your child learn short-term planning skills, consider the following:

- Give your child a part of the plan to arrange or discover by herself or take the lead in planning for—such as the clothes she'll wear or the best neighborhood places to walk the new puppy.

- Encourage games and activities that involve strategy and teamwork among siblings and/or the whole family, such as treasure hunts.

- Don't rush her. Allow her time to work out what she wants and to plan for it. Don't expect her ideas to be wholly rational and don't mock her if they're not. If something she's planned for won't work, explain why and make some suggestions for what would.

• Do what you say you are going to do, or let her know when plans have changed. Her emotional security depends on knowing that the people she idealizes are trustworthy.

• Don't expect a child under age four to be happy about putting off the good stuff; just explain that it's sometimes necessary.

GETTING TO *YES!*

Ultimately, optimism is a lifelong habit that is very largely about what we call "Getting to Yes!" "Yes! I can build a Lego house!" "Yes! I can do a somersault!" "Yes! I can make Mommy smile!" It's about upbeat confidence, realistically appraising what you can and can't do, not allowing one setback to deter you, and getting recognition for your competence from those who matter to you.

Optimism and resilience arise from succeeding even after setbacks, sometimes major ones. Javier, who was born with a disability that robbed him of the use of his right (and dominant) arm, developed a love of tennis—probably because both of his parents played the game. Instead of telling him he couldn't play, his parents, and later his teachers, encouraged him. As a preschooler, he hit thousands of balls across the net to his patient parents. When he got older and entered competitions, he lost many games on the way to mastery, but his parents never stopped encouraging him and he never stopped practicing. He developed a wicked underarm serve using only his left arm and, eventually, began to develop his unique island of competence and win games even with people who didn't have disabilities. He never got to Wimbledon, but with support and persistence he did get to Yes!

With the HAPPY principles, you give your child the basis for many Yes! experiences and a lifelong Yes! outlook.

13

OVERCOMING ATTENTION DEFICIT DISORDERS WITHOUT DRUGS

◉

The current concern over antidepressants for young children was fore-shadowed by the enormous and still growing controversy over the routine prescription of amphetamines such as Ritalin for attention deficit disorder (ADD) and attention deficit hyperactivity disorder (ADHD).

In 2004, Medco, the largest prescription benefit manager in the United States, reported a 369 percent increase in ADD/ADHD drug prescriptions for young children in the previous five years. Many researchers are dubious about the value of these drugs and highly concerned about their side effects, including loss of appetite, sleeplessness, psychosis (when taken in large doses), and depression, which can show up even years after stopping the amphetamines.[1]

There is growing speculation that these "disorders" are not a mental illness at all, but simply an expression of childhood or, in some cases, the way that depression and anxiety show up in boys. Because our society can't cope with the energy and high demands of some children, we are medicating their childhoods away.

THE DIAGNOSIS DILEMMA

In 2000, the National Institutes of Health (NIH) stated that the diversity of opinions about ADD/ADHD "raises questions concerning the literal existence of the disorder, whether it can be reliably diagnosed." Dr. Peter Jensen, from the National Institute of Mental Health (NIMH), added that ADD/ADHD remains of "unproven" status, which "should give pause to both researchers and clinicians who may have reified ADHD as a 'thing' or 'true entity' (rather than a *working hypothesis*)."[2]

Few of the many studies attempting to prove ADD/ADHD to be a neurological disorder have shown it to be anything other than a collection of seemingly related symptoms, which is why it is so easily misdiagnosed. There may well be a real neurological basis for some cases of the disorder, but this would appear from the studies to be fairly rare.

According to the psychiatrist's "bible," the *Diagnostic and Statistical Manual of Mental Disorders* (DSM IV), the ADD/ADHD child has a combination of several symptoms, which include impulsiveness, difficulty concentrating and completing tasks, forgetfulness, seeming not to listen when spoken to, being easily distractible, frequent fidgeting, and "excessive" running, climbing, or talking. This range of symptoms could apply to almost any child, particularly any preschool boy.[3] Some children diagnosed with ADD/ADHD are just exceptionally intelligent and understimulated. These symptoms could also be present in a child with depression, anxiety, bipolar disorder (manic depression), hypoglycemia, and dyslexia, or a range of other problems for which ADD/ADHD treatments are not only inappropriate but can also be dangerous.

The American Pediatric Association (APA) strongly suggests that pediatricians do not make a diagnosis of ADD/ADHD after just one session. Don't accept a diagnosis of ADD/ADHD without a series of sessions with a professional highly trained in this area, and even then be sure to get a second opinion. Resist pressure from day-care providers and teachers to medicate your child.

MEDICATING CHILDHOOD

Boys are much more frequently diagnosed with ADD/ADHD than girls (according to the U.S. Department of Health and Human Services, the ratio is about 4:1[4]), and many of its "symptoms" are in fact behaviors that prepared Stone Age boys for their role as hunters and are still embedded in their genes. A young apprentice hunter had to be very active, fast, strong, and curious. He needed to be "hyperalert" to any sign of danger and have a short, roving attention rather than a fixed focus most of the time. He learned to be a hunter by observing everything, experimenting with his senses, clambering over rocks, climbing trees, and playing energetic chasing and hiding games, not necessarily by words and certainly not by reading or watching TV. Boys from the Stone Age did not have to watch out for the good china or valuable antiques, follow complicated instructions, or sit still for long periods.

Yet boys are forced to remain indoors for much of the day; prevented from being boisterous; told to be quiet and calm; and punished, sometimes severely, for simply doing what their genes dictate. In his book *Darwinian Happiness*, biopsychologist Bjørn Grinde writes: "Rough-and-tumble play is an important innate behavioral tendency, and to suppress this activity is [a discord between our environment and our genes], and can have unwarranted consequences."[5] According to Grinde, Ritalin and similar amphetamine drugs simply reduce natural playfulness.[6] These drugs—and even the depression they can engender—make young children more compliant and easier to fit into a busy schedule, a day-care routine, or a crowded classroom.

Although girls also suffer from enforced inactivity and suppression, they are wired differently than boys for their original role as mothers and gatherers. Being better at communication and responsive to others' moods and (which, perhaps through social conditioning) often quieter and more eager to please authorities often gives them a large advantage in day care and classrooms.

Overcoming ADD/ADHD Behavior

Suppression of natural behaviors can exacerbate them, as anyone who has had to cope with young children after they've been made to sit still inside all day can attest. While much of ADD/ADHD is overdiagnosed, some children really do suffer from extreme forms of these symptoms, which usually have their origin in the child's emotional and physical environment—for example, trauma, poor parenting styles, insufficient maternal attachment, and a harmful diet. In fact, because of the links between behavioral problems and deficient early connection to the mother, some researchers have called ADD "an attachment deficit disorder."[7]

In a major article in the *Medical Journal of Australia*, Drs. George Halasz and Alasdair Vance of Australia's Monash University Medical Centre pleaded for greater understanding of the environmental factors behind the problem and advocated nondrug, family-centered approaches.[8]

No pill addresses the underlying causes of ADD/ADHD. The most that Ritalin and its pharmacological cousins can do is to clamp down on some symptoms. But most of these symptoms can be overcome without the use of drugs and with consistent application of five amazingly simple principles.

1. Patience

2. Boundaries

3. Play

4. Nature

5. Time

Cultivate Patience

Many of the symptoms of ADD/ADHD are the result of lack of patience and understanding on the part of parents, day-care providers, and teachers.

From the age of ten months, Elijah seemed different. Unlike his older sisters, who were their parents' pride and joy, he was slow to speak in full sentences and threw tantrums over his frustration at his being unable to communicate. He got upset over any change in routine, was easily startled, and became enraged when his desires were thwarted. Elijah's mother, Ruby, was a well-known TV personality who spent a great deal of time at the studio. Leonard, his father, was a successful businessman, spent little time at home, and wanted Elijah to grow up to be like him—smart, quick, and rich. When Elijah didn't match his father's expectations, Leonard was disappointed and then irritated. Following their parents' lead, Elijah's sisters snubbed and teased their little brother, which made him more easily upset, awkward, and slow to learn. Elijah's day-care providers, who watched after the little boy five days a week during the parents' regular working hours and often well beyond, found him disruptive, unfocused, and hyperactive and asked that he be medicated. After a brief consultation, a pediatrician diagnosed ADD/ADHD and prescribed Ritalin.

After a year had passed and Elijah's symptoms had worsened despite treatment, another pediatrician referred his parents to Bob, who persuaded them to give the then four-year-old the patience and understanding he so desperately needed. Bob showed them how to deal with Elijah's frustration over simple tasks by "chunking down" a direction or activity into smaller pieces he could grasp and waiting until he indicated that he understood each piece before moving on. For example, getting dressed became a ritualized step-by-step process of putting on undies ("Good. Ready?"), shirt ("Good. Ready?"), pants ("Good. Ready?"), socks ("Good. Ready?"), and shoes ("Yes!"). The family came up with a tune to match the activities, which never failed to delight the little boy. As his confidence in the simple job of getting dressed grew, so did his ability to cope with frustration and new tasks.

Bob also advised the parents to let Elijah tackle tasks in his own time whenever possible, without trying to do them for him or hurrying him. Studies have shown that, by and large, children do much better if their parents allow them to discover things for themselves and without giving unnecessary advice or help.[9] With an attention-deficit or hyperactive child, this is especially true. Issuing commands or rushing them leads to disengagement and a seeming lack of attention.

Moreover, children under age four have no real sense of time in the adult meaning of the world. Getting angry at your toddler because he is "late" is counterproductive. Even "Be ready in ten minutes!" is meaningless—to him ten minutes is all the time in the world! He gets his concept of time through routine events—breakfast, preschool, lunch, play, dinner, bathtime, story-time, bed—which all tend to happen in a regular sequence and at the same time each day.

Bob also pointed out that Elijah wasn't stupid or even unable to pay attention, but like most children under four, he had difficulty with complex decisions, impulse control, and abstract concepts.[10] When his parents assumed he was unable to concentrate or trying to annoy them by insisting a white baseball was brown, for example, Bob explained that because the boy was wearing sunglasses the ball was indeed brown to him. Since young children have no concept of a permanent state, the ball was brown until he removed the glasses, when it was white.

Elijah's parents learned to help him make decisions by neither over-whelming him with options or dictating only one possibility. Instead they gave him limited choices—orange or grapefruit juice rather than offering him any drink in the supermarket, or walking in the park versus around the block.

Patience paid off with Elijah and, along with the following techniques, resulted in a dramatic change in just a few months. "It's been hard work," admits Ruby, who cut down her work hours in order to spend more time with her son. "And there were times when we back-slipped and I got really dis-couraged. But when we didn't lose our patience or determination, we began to notice enormous shifts. We're happy to report that these changes have now lasted for about a year."

Tip: If your child has ADD/ADHD symptoms, set up routines and stick to them as much as possible. Explain any deviations ahead of time so he can adjust.

MAINTAIN FIRM BOUNDARIES

After patience, what a child who seems hyperactive needs almost more than anything else is firm and predictable boundaries. He gets his sense of self-control through the consistent external restraints you put in place. You have to be very clear about what behaviors you will and won't allow and ready to have those boundaries tested time after time. When you discipline an attention deficit or hyperactive child, you must do so calmly and, whenever possible, right away so that he clearly sees cause and effect.

You and your partner should work out what's most important to you and your child's welfare and focus initially on changing those behaviors. Don't try to control everything; the fewer things your child has to bear in mind at any time, the better.

You do need to be very firm around behavior that can actually cause ADD/ADHD-like symptoms, such as excessive television viewing and diet. A 2004 study, carried out by researchers at the University of Washington in Seattle and published in the journal *Pediatrics*, showed that the likelihood of a child's developing ADD/ADHD rose in direct proportion to the amount of television he watched as a toddler.[11] Most researchers recommend that toddlers and preschoolers be allowed to watch less than two hours of TV per day.

A wide range of natural and processed foods have been implicated in attention deficit problems. Those most often mentioned in research papers include sugar, food additives, and caffeine. Diets that eliminate these have been shown to be as effective as drugs in reducing ADD/ADHD symptoms,[12] and yet in recent years studies have shown that the consumption of substances that limit a child's ability to concentrate or be attentive has increased.[13] Make a project of finding healthy, natural foods your child likes, and make sure the whole family follows a similarly healthy eating plan.

Don't forget the Family Powwow when you set these all-important rules. Following many of the same rules yourselves (too much TV and junk food aren't good for you or other family members either!) and letting your child have a say about consequences can help him feel he's not being picked on arbitrarily. If you ban junk food for your child but keep foods around that he can't eat or consume them in front of him, you're asking for problems.

It's also very important for parents to have clearly understood boundaries with each other. Parental arguing and other problems in the home environment are some of the prime causes of ADD/ADHD behavior.[14] A study conducted by researchers at Belgium's Catholic University of Leuven found that children whose mothers had been subjected to marital and other stressors during the first twenty-two weeks of pregnancy were far more prone to ADD/ADHD.[15] New guidelines for pediatricians call for them to ask about a child's home environment as part of their normal intake session.

Tip: If there are particular places such as the supermarket or mall where your child tends to feel overwhelmed and be disruptive, try to avoid taking him there until your new regime of firm, clear rules has been consistently applied for a while and has had a chance to have an effect.

PROMOTE ACTIVE PLAY

Play is how young children prepare themselves for adulthood and relationships. Professor Anthony Pellegrini of the University of Minnesota is among a growing number of researchers who have linked ADD/ADHD to a lack of exercise and, more important, to a child not having the opportunity to play.

In a 2002 report, Pellegrini blamed the rise in the disorder and antisocial behavior on the increase in classroom activities at the expense of recess and breaks. What is happening in schools is mirrored in kindergartens and in homes, where even very young children are increasingly kept indoors and required to practice academic skills.[16]

To enhance early cognitive development, socialization, and learning as well as ward off ADD/ADHD, allow plenty of time for physical activities, especially with the family and other kids.

Tip: So the kids can still get to bed on time, make sure Dad has enough time during the day and early evening to engage in the rough-and-tumble play children crave. Excitement right before bedtime will make it difficult for a child to settle, and keeping to a sleep routine is especially important for a child with ADD/ADHD.

SURROUND YOUR CHILD WITH NATURE

"Our findings indicate that exposure to ordinary natural settings in the course of common after-school and weekend activities may be widely effective in reducing attention deficit symptoms in children," said environment sciences and psychology professor Frances Kuo of the University of Illinois, in a press release about her landmark 2004 study. Kuo noted that simply being in nature "may offer a way to help manage ADHD symptoms that is readily available, doesn't have any stigma associated with it, doesn't cost anything, and doesn't have any side effects—except maybe splinters!"[17]

It's not surprising that separation from nature is increasingly implicated in depression and ADD/ADHD, since both problems have largely the same origins, are often present in the same children, and, in some cases, may be the same disorder.

We have seen ADD/ADHD symptoms dramatically improve when a pet, especially a dog, is added to the household. Particularly good breeds are gentle but still playful, protective, and robust, such as a golden retriever, collie, Labrador, or many mixed breeds. Many studies have shown that just being around a dog (or cat) reduces stress, and under parental guidance, they can encourage a sense of responsibility in kids.[18]

When Danny's mother came to see Alicia for her own depression, she brought her five-year-old to the suburban New York offices we had at the time. Danny had been diagnosed with ADD/ADHD, and his mother's depression was severely triggered by her perceived "failure" to bring up a calm, obedient child.

Danny was immediately taken with our good-tempered golden retriever–collie cross, Biscuit, whom we had rescued from a local pound. Alicia suggested that Danny and Biscuit take some time to get acquainted during the mother's session under the watchful eye of our receptionist, and soon the pair were romping vigorously together on the front lawn. When Danny's mother finished the session, she found her "hyperactive" son quietly sitting with the large golden dog, entirely focused on stroking his fur and speaking softly to him. "My God! I've never seen him that calm," she whispered, as if afraid to break the spell. "Tomorrow we get a dog!"

Additional ways to expose your child to the healing power of nature include:

- Take him regularly to a park or nature reserve to play or walk.

- Give him a room that looks out over trees or grass. If this isn't possible, put up pictures of nature.

- Visit a nature center where the exhibits stimulate children's curiosity about the natural world or pet store or petting zoo where he can cuddle the animals.

- If you have a pet, demonstrate the love you have for the animal and the joy of being with this family member. Set clear instructions around how to treat your pet and give your child a role in caring for it.

DEVOTE YOUR TIME

All of these principles will enormously help relieve, if not banish, your child's symptoms, and they cost relatively little or nothing. Yet they all require one thing: time. Your time, with your child. Time to understand what is really going on and what caused the problem; time to learn the patience to deal with a child who is overactive but who may well also be gifted; time to set and maintain boundaries; time to play and invent new and interesting games; time to go for outings into the country or through the park; time to choose a pet and show your child how to care for and handle it. Just time. It's the most important gift you can give your child.

14

DEPRESSION-PROOFING
THE BODY

◉

Depression is a malady not just of the mind, but of the body. In fact, the separation of those two aspects of our experience, of our consciousness, is a prime cause of many of today's problems.

Depression lowers the immune system and can show up as physical illness even in small children. It is related to poor body image and eating disorders from anorexia to obesity, the primary health danger facing children and the most common form of a child's self-destructive behavior. One of the ways that childhood trauma reinforces depression is through lodging in the body; restricting posture, movement, and breathing; and sending ongoing messages of danger to the brain.

As an example of just how closely mind and body are linked, consider that scientists have discovered a number of brains ("peripheral nervous systems"), including one in the stomach. This belly brain consists of one hundred billion cells and may store information on physical reactions to mental processes and give out signals that influence later decisions. It may also be responsible for "gut reactions," such as joy, fear, or sadness, or intuitive "gut feelings." It's possible to cycle between being depressed in one's mood (sad, hopeless) and one's gut (irritable bowel, a chronic "stomachache").

Promoting your child's positive connection to her body is one of the most important ways you depression-proof her future. It depends not only on your interactions with her, but on your feelings about your own body and the positive—or negative—attitudes and behaviors you model.

NEGATIVE BODY IMAGE

Negative body self-image and eating disorders from anorexia to obesity—even ones that show up many years later—have their origins in parenting styles and can begin in infancy. Research by Alfonso Troisi and colleagues in the Department of Neurosciences at the University of Rome has shown that children who have not formed a secure attachment to their principal caregiver (usually their mothers) are more likely to develop poor body image and eating disorders.[1] (A close mother/child bond will also delay the onset of teen sexual experimentation.[2])

If a child feels she's being abandoned—by being sent too early to day care, for example, or not given enough undistracted time with parents—then, over time, she will develop an obsessive need to control her body as a way of overcoming the pain of separation.[3] She may also regard food as the only source of love. If she doesn't feel physically safe because of physical punishment, violence in the house, bullying, or having sexual boundaries transgressed, she may starve herself so as to deny her sexuality or overeat to create a cushioning barrier of fat.

Recent research carried out by Hayley Dohnt of Flinders University in South Australia has found that girls as young as age six can exhibit eating disorders, believing that they need to be thin to be popular.[4] This kind of belief begins with parental attitudes and then is reinforced by peers at school as well as by the media.

In fact, your child can catch your negative body image. If your five-year-old sees you pinching your flesh in front of a mirror and muttering how ugly you look, you may be setting her up for an eating disorder. You may also be spreading depression, since mood disorders and eating disorders are causally linked.[5]

What you say is as important as what you do. For example, if you tell your son that he "ought to be bigger" (or allow siblings to tease him about his size) you may be setting him up later for what is called "bigorexia"—a preoccupation with muscle mass. And, as Kenyon College psychology professor Linda Smolak and her team discovered, whatever critical remarks you (or others in your hearing) make to your daughter about her weight or about her body generally can have profound negative consequences for her body image, her self-identity, and future eating disorders.[6] If you make her feel fat, for instance, she may embark on a lifetime of dieting and bingeing that inexorably drives the scale upward.

By adolescence, the main predictors of obesity are depression, engaging in radical weight-control behaviors, and obese parents, according to researchers from the University of Texas and the Oregon Research Institute. These factors were far more predictive of obesity than exercise or fat consumption.[7]

Tip: Your child is beautiful no matter what her size. You can suggest that she eat less, or better, or forbid certain foods—as long as you explain why. But critical remarks never help.

PROGRAMMED BY TV

The medical establishment has long linked TV to eating disorders and poor body image, yet children are watching more TV today than ever. "Keep toddlers away from television," pleaded Dr. Michael McDowell of the Royal Australasian College of Physicians in a 2004 policy statement. He added, "The amount of money spent by large commercial organizations on understanding children's development for the purpose of exploiting them is now more than universities spend [on child development studies]."[8]

Advertisers target children, encouraging them to buy fattening foods—soft drinks, ice cream, candies, burgers—while at the same time both ads and programs feature impossibly thin women and muscular men. Writing in the medical journal *The Lancet*, Dr. David Ludwig of Boston's Children's Hospital stated: "Measures to limit television viewing in childhood and ban food advertisements aimed at children are warranted, before another generation is programmed to become obese."[9]

Children under age six don't have the ability to tell fact from fiction on TV or the discernment to separate advertisements from programs. The rapidly changing images in commercials appeal to them, and they accept what is said as truth. It's your job to help her to make this distinction *and*, at the same time, reinforce your own positive values.

Four-year-old Molly's parents asked Alicia for help with her demanding behavior, anger, and obesity. Molly's mother and father both worked in jobs requiring them to put in long and irregular hours. Molly's caretakers allowed her to eat junk food because it was easier than setting limits. When her parents came home, they guiltily brought Molly fattening treats. However, the greatest problem was TV. Even when they were home, from Molly's infancy her parents allowed the TV set to be her caregiver for hours at a time. She could quote advertisements verbatim and got very angry if her parents didn't buy the brand-name soft drinks and candies she had been "programmed" to desire.

There is growing concern that very young children's sexuality is also being programmed inappropriately. Music video clips displaying heavily made-up and scantily clad teen singers are dispersed with children's programming, and provocative clothes are marketed to preschoolers.

Tip: When you first cut down on your child's viewing, be prepared for rage, tantrums, and a test of wills. It's important not to give in. Hide the remote. Don't have a TV set in her room, and restrict your own viewing until after she's gone to bed.

YOUR DEPRESSION AND HER OBESITY

One of the reasons depressed kids watch more TV than others is that they are likely to have depressed parents, particularly mothers, who do so. Several recent studies have shown a direct link between parental, especially maternal, depression and children's obesity (as well as children's depression).[10] In our practice, we also have found a strong causal connection between parental depression and a number of eating disorders in children. The behaviors and attitudes toward the body that go with depression—lack of physical exercise, excessive TV watching, overeating, low self-esteem, body hatred, violence, and threatening behavior—breed depression.

For example, children of depressed mothers watch, on average, an hour more of television a day than those whose mothers are not depressed, according to a study presented at the 2001 conference of the North American Association for the Study of Obesity by Dr. Hillary Burdette of the Children's Hospital Medical Center of Cincinnati. Dr. Burdette and others believe that, in order to effectively deal with a child's weight problem, physicians and others should focus on the mother's well-being. Says Dr. Burdette, "As health professionals, when we tell moms to turn off the television and they don't follow our advice, we need to find out what's going on there."[11]

Tip: If your child shows signs of becoming obese, maybe the first thing to do is seek help for yourself.

TEACHING GOOD BODY IMAGE
AND AWARENESS

According to associate professor Stacey Tantleff-Dunn, "The key is to help people develop realistic expectations about their appearance, as well as the appearance of others, and avoid buying into ideals that are impossible or unhealthy to attain."[12]

Gentle and affectionate physical contact is a vital grounding for good connection to the body, and yet our modern lifestyle limits opportunities for contact. Allowing your infant to sleep or rest with you and carrying her in a sling or special baby-wearer are some ways you can increase this highly beneficial closeness. At around five months, your baby realizes that she is separate from her mother, that she has arms, legs, toes, and fingers that are all hers. She becomes fascinated and plays with them endlessly. You can encourage this emerging body awareness and autonomy by placing an unbreakable mirror in front of her. She'll soon be riveted by her appearance and come to recognize her face.

The way you touch your baby is extremely important. If you are often upset with yourself and in a hurry, you may find yourself handling her impatiently or even abruptly. If, on the other hand, you take time to gently hold and appreciate her body, so, eventually, will she. Massaging her feet and hands and stroking her back and tummy not only provide comfort and lay the groundwork for self-esteem but offer beneficial stimulation to the nervous system. Say things like "how beautiful you are" or "what lovely hands." Of course, she won't understand the words, but she'll comprehend the tone of approval in your voice.

From five months to a year, you might stand in front of a mirror with your baby and say things like "Where's Mommy?" "Where's Baby?" "Where's Mommy's tummy?" "Where's Baby's tummy?" playing a pointing game as you do so.

Be aware of, and don't seem put off by, your baby's early signs of sexuality. Baby boys frequently get erections and will even seem to masturbate. Baby girls will get damp in their sexual areas just like a grown woman and may even show fascination with this area of their bodies. Let them be, this is a normal development. If you show disapproval by voice or action, you may engender shame and do great harm.

By eighteen months, your child really understands that she's a separate individual. Praise her motor skills and the way she uses her body. From two to six years old, she wants to show you how fast she can run and how high she can jump. She experiments and seems to have no sense of danger. Sometimes her high jinks are frightening. Try to avoid constant displays of alarm, admonishments, and warnings. Persistent repetition of phrases like "You must slow down!" or "You're going to fall!" can be interpreted by her as "My legs run too fast" or "I'm clumsy." These can be the early seeds of a negative body image. The trick is to get her to understand that it's her actions that are the problem, not her body. Explain to her that "if you run so fast around your toys, you may trip."

Along with her pride in her newfound physical abilities goes an intense curiosity about her own and other people's bodies—why boys stand to urinate while she sits down, for example. She will be curious about parts of her body she can't normally see and will twist around to examine her bottom in the mirror. Again, like your baby's early sexuality, this is normal behavior and your negative reactions can be harmful.

As she grows, she may become intrigued by her mommy's looks and want to dress up to look like her, just as her brother may want to put on his dad's clothes or practice shaving. By age four or five, they'll also want to resemble their same-sex friends, wear the same clothes, even carry the same backpacks. They're becoming aware of gender differences. They're very sensitive to criticism by peers and by you. Phrases such as "No more for you, your tummy's big enough as it is!" or "If you keep growing like this, I'm going to go broke buying you clothes!" can make your child feel bad about her body.

Other no-nos at this age are instructions to "stand up straight," "mind your posture," or "put your shoulders back!" Children need to find their own way of standing, sitting, and moving. There is, in fact, no "right way" to stand or hold yourself. Mostly they will take their cues from the way you hold yourself and, to a lesser extent, from their playmates. Also, their bodies will take on a defensive stance in relation to danger or criticism—and further criticism about their posture will just reinforce the problem.

Tip: Never criticize your own body or that of your partner. After all, your child wants to look like you, and sending a message that you're unhappy with your body will make her unhappy with hers.

HEALTHY EXERCISE IN NATURE

Studies have shown that an increasing "greening" of children's lives and activities is a powerful antidepressant as well as a cure for attention deficit problems and an aid to learning and thinking skills.[13]

For young children, exercise and physical activities that involve the family make the most impact and can lead to a healthy attitude. Your child won't think much of keeping her body fit if you don't, and going to the gym or a yoga class and excluding her isn't the message you want to send, either.

For your child, exercise isn't about getting fit or keeping slim or muscular, it's about fun, experimentation, and curiosity. It's about exploring her physical abilities as well as her world, nature, and relationships.

Nature gives a child a chance to exercise her curiosity as well as her body; to explore different surfaces to run and walk on, climb over, and hang from; and thus master new motor skills and gain confidence. As she grows up, she will be more likely to remain centered in her body, more present to the moment and connected to her authentic self.

A regular walk of twenty minutes or more each day in natural surroundings can be an exercise in awareness for the whole family. How many changes can you notice? What's different? What does it feel like to walk, skip, and run? This awareness can take you or your child out of the depressed self and facilitate a connection not only to nature but to your innate spirituality in much the same way as meditation.

And instilling a love of movement and nature will give your child a powerful, lifelong antidote to depression.

15

MANAGING DIFFICULT TRANSITIONS

◉

All depression involves a loss—of a beloved person or of something less tangible, such as one's role, sense of belonging, status, safety, or trust. For a child, all transitions entail a loss, whether it be of a parent or sibling through death or divorce; the parents' undivided attention when a new sibling comes along; a parent's emotional presence due to depression or addiction; or even the loss of a house, neighborhood, and friends due to relocation. The child's ability to survive these transitions without lasting damage and depression depends on the strength of his remaining primary relationships. If his parents (or parent substitutes) show by their actions that they care for him and can be counted on, he will have trust; if they show that they can get along, he will have safety; if they are clear about their appropriate expectations and values, he will have belonging; if they explain events in terms he can understand, he will gradually come to acceptance.

MAGICAL THINKING AND MAGICAL GUILT

One of the reasons that loss and transitions can have such a devastating effect on very young children is that they don't perceive reality as we do. Toddler and preschool years are a time of "magical thinking," when your child finds it difficult to separate fantasy from reality. Magical thinking can be delightful—a visit from an imaginary friend. It can also be dangerous—a two-year-old deciding to fly down the steps like Superman.

Part of magical thinking is egocentricity—your little angel thinks he is the center of the universe and all things either involve him or are caused by his actions or thoughts. If someone dies or gets ill, he may believe that his nasty thoughts are responsible. If he gets sick, he may believe that his wickedness has brought this upon himself as punishment.

So when something goes wrong, whether it's a divorce or a job loss, a child can feel an overwhelming sense of guilt and shame, leading to regressive behaviors such as bed-wetting; poor learning skills; difficulty making friends and playing with other children; and poor self-esteem. His deep sense of deserving punishment can even create illness through a lowering of the immune system. According to June Price Tangney, psychology professor at George Mason University, lifelong consequences of shame can include "a range of potentially destructive motivations, defenses, interpersonal behaviors, and psychological symptoms" including, of course, depression.[1]

Parental depression is a significant factor in how the child's guilt develops and is expressed. If his parents aren't depressed, his guilt will take on themes of responsibility and reparation (trying to make things better), which may actually aid him in making social connections later and ameliorating guilty feelings. If, on the other hand, the parents, particularly the mother, suffer from depression, the child's guilt may be self-destructive, distorted, and unresolved.[2]

Obviously, two main ways of helping your child cope with loss are to explain it in terms he can understand and to constantly reassure him that he has done nothing wrong. Also, if the loss is affecting you as well, get help for your depression. In this chapter, we outline some specific ways to help your child cope with three common types of loss: divorce, the arrival of a new sibling, and death.

Divorce and Separation

Each year more than a million young children in the United States experience the divorce of their parents.[3] About 25 percent of them will develop serious mental health problems as a result, twice the rate of children from continuously married families. Of the remaining 75 percent, many are at risk for lifelong emotional problems[4] and a shorter life expectancy.[5] A child's greatest fear is abandonment, and the breakup of his family will create a sense of loss and abandonment that can be as great as if a parent had died.

A U.S. and U.K. team of researchers led by Thomas O'Connor of the Psychiatric Institute in London recently found that divorce also seems to turn on a genetic switch that causes problems in academic performance in the children of divorced parents.[6]

There's nothing new or shameful about divorce. Marriages in Stone Age times lasted, on average, about seven years (about the same length as today in the United States), and a woman then could expect to go through four husbands in a lifetime. The big difference between then and now is that in hunter-gatherer times people lived in small, tightly knit communities and the couple remained within the band even when marriages dissipated. What's more, the whole band, not just the children's biological parents, played an active role in nurturing its progeny. In this context, there was little or no damage to the children.[7]

In developed societies, there's no longer a supportive tribe to soften the blow. Divorce is often damaging to parents, and this in turn affects children. In a 2002 study that many researchers found surprising, researchers in Finland discovered that divorced men were more likely to suffer from anxiety and depression and an increase in health-related problems such as smoking and alcoholism, while women fared better.[8] On the other hand, divorced women, particularly those caring for young children, are more likely to struggle financially.

Young children of divorced parents fare worst of all. O'Connor and his team found that children of divorced parents had more behavioral and emotional problems (aggressive behavior, delinquency, depression, anxiety, and withdrawal) and poorer social adjustment than children whose parents stayed together. As these children reached their teens, they also reported earlier drug use than children whose parents did not divorce.[9]

Divorce often creates guilt in young children, who believe subconsciously that they caused the fighting, drove their parents to separate, and are so evil that they deserve to be abandoned and punished by the split. This guilt can affect all their behaviors and self-image. In later life, they are likely to seek out abandoners as romantic partners or drive people away from them.

The most important things you can do to help shield your child from the painful effects of divorce are foster a warm and empathic relationship with him, maintain consistent discipline and boundaries, and avoid exposing him to negative interactions with your ex.[10] The following strategies can also lessen the damage of divorce:

- Opt for joint custody. Children who spend equal time with both parents fare better than those whose mother (or father) has sole custody. If parents are not hostile, the arrangement can work out well for all concerned—the parents have their freedom and the children proximity to them both.[11]

- Live within an hour's drive of your child. Studies have shown that the closer you live, the better he does.[12]

- Do not engage in a competition with your ex-spouse for your child's love.

- Never belittle your ex in your child's presence. Rather, praise your ex.

- Don't use your child as a go-between with your ex-spouse. Clear boundaries and Needs-Based Dialogue will help keep your relationship civil.

- Come to an agreement with your ex about the rules of both houses—kids need to have consistency, not one set of rules for one place and another set for the other place.

- Be very clear about what you need from your ex logistically, financially, and emotionally in order for you to make a worthwhile contribution to your children's welfare. Make sure you know exactly what your ex needs from you.

- Always do what you tell your child you're going to do.

- Try to keep your child in the loop about what's happening with you from the time you decide to divorce—minus the nasty bits.

- Continue to have Family Powwows with your ex and child to iron out problems.

In other words, behave as closely as possible to how your Stone Age ancestors lived millennia ago when divorce and separation did not have the destructive impact they do today.

INTRODUCING A SECOND CHILD

We've all heard about sibling rivalry, but few realize that one of the reasons the addition of another child is so difficult for the firstborn is that the whole family tends to be in upheaval. Parents tend not to give as much thought to the impact on their lives of a second child as they did to the first, although that impact is usually just as great, if not more so. Two children are not as easy as one, and a lack of planning and foresight may add to an already high level of stress and even to depression and marital discord.

Lack of sleep is a big problem for parents of two young children. As psychologist and author Dr. Susan Bartell says, "Substantial and unrelenting sleep deprivation can make it difficult to parent adequately, can affect memory, and is strongly correlated with depression."[13] For Mom, the arrival of a new child can mean even less "downtime," time to herself or with friends. She may feel trapped and even resentful of the demands her toddler makes on her, not understanding that his needs for her attention are just as great as before.

However, the impact may be greater still on the father. Says Bartell, "It is rare that a father's feelings about his role as a parent are taken into account as one of the deciding factors [in having a second child]—after all, he's not carrying the baby or giving birth and, despite societal changes, the mother is still seen as the primary nurturer. However, it is usually the father, not the mother, whose role is most drastically affected by the second child. When the second child is born, Dad is often expected to become the primary nurturer for the older child."[14] He may relish this role, or he may resent it and unconsciously take these feelings out on the child.

Meanwhile, the first child has not stopped needing Mother's nurture and, no matter how skillful and willing Dad is, he will feel an acute sense of loss. Even if he seems very independent, he may well perceive the new baby as a threat to his special relationship with Mom. No longer the center of his mother's attention, he is, as psychologists say, "dethroned," cast out of his former supreme position.

Obviously, it's vital that you prepare as thoroughly for the birth of your second child as the first, revising your Parenting Priority Plan in light of the changed circumstances and ensuring a minimum of distress for yourselves and your firstborn. In addition, there are some things you can do directly to mitigate your first child's sense of loss.

Libby and Sean came to see Alicia for advice regarding their four-year-old son, Patrick, a few months after the arrival of their new child. Before his sibling's arrival, Patrick had seemed enthusiastic about having a baby sister. He took a great interest in the swelling of Libby's stomach, gladly went on shopping expeditions to get new things for the nursery, and was constantly asking questions.

"But as soon as Kimberly arrived, he changed," Libby told Alicia. "He still seems interested in the baby, but he occasionally wets his bed, which he hasn't done for ages, he cries a lot, he seems more like a two-year-old than a four-year-old. He also doesn't sleep much and comes into our room and wakes me up."

"And the tantrums!" Sean exclaimed. "Constant tantrums, over anything. Not so much with me, but with Libby. Of course I get angry with him, who wouldn't! I need him to stop."

Alicia explained that Sean's getting angry with Patrick only reinforced his son's feeling that Kimberly had become the favorite and worsened his regressive behaviors. "You can't expect him to like the situation," Alicia told them. "Before the birth, he saw Kimberly rather like a new toy for him to play with. He didn't understand that this was a real person with whom he would have to share his mother. The reality was a shock to him. The behaviors that he's showing at the moment are perfectly normal and in no way indicate that he won't come to love Kimberly."

Alicia's suggestions to Libby and Sean were:

- Allow Patrick to express his feelings appropriately. Validate and encourage him to talk about them—he has a right to feel upset. If he has to repress his anger, it will turn inward and, possibly, become depression.

- At the same time, maintain your boundaries. Let him know which actions are acceptable and which are not (complaining about Kimberly to you is OK, since he needs to let off steam; playing roughly or hurting the baby isn't).

- Show him that you love him. Give time to him, even if it means taking some time away from the baby.

- Give him a role in dealing with the baby. Being "Mom's helper" and "big brother" may involve lending a hand at bath time and showing baby how to hold her rattle. Praise him lavishly for doing so.

- Explain what is going on, making him as much a part of the process as possible. As you feed, bathe, and care for the baby, explain how you nurtured him when he was little. At the same time, you can point out that while babies are cute, they can't do all the things a four-year-old can. Don't tell your older child that he's a big boy now and should "grow up."

- Try to do things with your baby and toddler at the same time, such as sitting on the floor and breast-feeding baby in a sling while you read a story or play with your older child.

- Be patient. Before reacting, take a deep breath and count to ten!

- Express your frustrations *to* each other—not *at* the kids.

With these tools, Libby and Sean were able to understand and cope with Patrick's natural reaction to Kimberly's arrival. Patrick came to see the new baby as a family project that he was intimately involved in, rather than a rival competing for his parents' love. After a while, his regressive behaviors ceased.

A DEATH IN THE FAMILY

Each year, approximately 4 percent of young children in the United States suffer the death of a parent.[15] Young children don't really understand the concept of death, so when someone dies they are likely to treat the loss as abandonment and react accordingly, often with profound and lifelong effects on mood and relationships. Children come to terms with the death of someone close to them in different ways, which largely depends on their stage of development (in the early years, a child will react far more strongly to losing his mother than his father or anyone else), whether another adult steps in to pick up the slack, and whether they are helped to understand what has happened.

Infants express grief predominantly as crying and irritability, poor sleep, variable appetite, hyperactivity, withdrawal, and increased vigilance. In infancy, the child will need consistent caretaking. If it's his mother who has died (or his father if he was the primary caretaker), another permanent caretaker must be immediately assigned. An infant must not be passed from caretaker to caretaker. Talking about death to a two-year-old is also a waste of time. A person is either there or they're not. A child suffering the loss of a parent needs lots of gentle touch rather than words. He needs holding, cuddling, and stroking.

Three- and four-year-old children have a capacity to remember the deceased. They do not, however, understand the process of dying and do not recognize that death is permanent. Rather, they see it as abandonment. Children may believe they have magical capacities that caused the death and that can make the person return. They may experience intense anxiety and insecurity about separations and are acutely attuned to the emotions of their caregivers. Similar to infants, they may express grief in emotions, sleeplessness, and regressive behavior.

A young child's sense of guilt and shame will also be affected by the way the death occurred. If the death was from a protracted illness, the grieving process may begin beforehand. He will have a chance to, in some way, come to terms with the expected loss, recover more quickly, and more readily understand that the event was not his fault. If, on the other hand, the loss was sudden, then the immediate shock may impede his functioning and throw him into a state of confusion, anxiety, and depression.[16] This is also true if the death is not adequately explained in terms a child can understand, or, even worse, if the family pretends it hasn't happened.

Maya told Bob with great sadness about the loss of her father thirty years ago when she was about five. "One day he just wasn't there. Mom said he'd gone away, and I thought that meant he'd be back and I just kept waiting and asking when he'd return. No one told me what really happened, or asked me how I felt—not my mother, not my aunt, not my grandpa. I loved Dad. I kept wondering what I'd done wrong, why he didn't come back to me. I prayed to God to send him home. I left notes for him saying I missed him.

"It was only in my late teens that I learned, quite by accident, that he'd committed suicide. They all lied to me. I haven't spoken to my mother since. But I can't seem to get on with my life, find someone to love, stop feeling sad and inadequate. It's like I'm waiting for my dad to come back, to tell me I'm OK."

As with Maya, a child's feelings can become frozen as a result of a death. He may seem not to grieve at all, as if his feelings have been put on hold. When the feelings about the person or how they died are ambiguous, perhaps involving anger, the result is "complicated grief," the most difficult to deal with and the most likely to lead to permanent depression, anxiety, or a tendency toward rage. Complicated grief can result from death as a result of murder, suicide, or accident; death that results in a social stigma such as death from AIDS or drug overdose; or death of an abusive, abandoning, or single parent.

Whatever the cause of death, you can help preschoolers (and even toddlers) in the following ways:

- Point out over and over again that the loved one did not choose to leave and abandon the child, but that there was a specific cause of death.

- Encourage a child older than age two to talk about his feelings. Try not to ask him questions that only need a "yes" or "no" response. Begin questions with "who," "what," "where," "why," or "how."

- Understand that a young child's attention span is very short, and time your discussion in relation to his cues. He may seem concerned about the loss and ask all sorts of questions one moment and go back to seemingly unconcerned play the next. This does not necessarily mean that he is recovering.

- Never ask a child who has suffered a major loss to "act like a man" or "be a big girl" and not cry. Your child needs to express the loss in order to recover. If he is forced or even encouraged to bury or deny his feelings, he may never cycle out of them, and another layer of shame will be added.

Sometimes complicated grief needs the input of a skilled therapist, working directly with the child, in order to uncover underlying issues. Remember, however, to consider getting help yourself, since your child will largely take his cues on how to react to a situation from you. As with any loss, if you are honestly dealing with your feelings around the situation, he can learn to as well.

16

TIPS FOR BLENDED
FAMILIES AND
SINGLE PARENTS

◉

U ntil recently, most couples living together were married, and the vast
majority of children resided with their biological parents. That this is
no longer true worries scholars such as James Q. Wilson, author of *The Marriage Problem: How Our Culture Has Weakened Families*. He and other
researchers believe that the fragmentation of the modern family has profound
implications for the welfare of children.[1] More than anything, a young child
needs stability, consistency, and the chance to form a strong attachment to a
caregiver. The lack of any of these can lead to depression and a range of other
problems—such as addiction and ongoing failure of relationships—that may
not show up until much later. Beside the traditional nuclear unit, modern
families include a single mother or father, sometimes living with their parents (multigenerational families), cohabiting parent families, and married
blended families.

For the child, however, the main factor in any family arrangement is the
quality and stability of the relationships.

BLENDED FAMILIES

Some researchers view the blended family as the next "traditional American family," and half of all U.S. children now live with at least one step-parent.[2] This situation poses enormous challenges to stepparents, and studies show that children living in stepfamily situations fare worse than those living with two biological parents, largely because second families tend to be less stable.[3] According to the U.S. Census Bureau (1990 figures, the latest available), 60 percent of all remarriages end in divorce; some studies indicate the rate is much higher. Why is this? Our ancestors may have heeded the "seven-year itch," but most post-hunter-gatherer couples without tribal support probably intend to stay together and find divorce painful. As you may recall from Chapter 4, we tend to unconsciously re-create the relationships our parents had with each other until we learn how to make more positive choices. If the parents' relationship was troubled, the child will probably find that all her major relationships are problematic.[4] Studies also show that people tend to marry those with similar (and thus often unstable) marital histories.[5]

Don't let the statistics get you down, however; there are plenty of successful blended families and no reason why yours won't be one of them. Raising children is challenging, and raising other people's children is even more challenging, but your love for each other is (hopefully) the reason you came together in the first place and remains the foundation of a happy household. Needs-Based Dialogue will ensure your relationship doesn't repeat old patterns and provide a good foundation for all the children.

When Susan and Ian married, soon after their respective divorces, each brought two children with them, including a four- and a six-year-old. The couple felt guilty about the failure of their first marriages and anxious about making the situation work for all the children. Says Susan: "We were trying so hard to keep the kids from jumping down each other's throats and make them happy that we ignored our own boundaries and needs, particularly as a couple. If one of us said no, they just started working on the other—or our exes. The kids could come into our bedroom at any time, and interrupt any discussion—and believe me, they did."

The strain showed up not only in the couple's relationship, which was rapidly deteriorating, but in Ian's mood, which began to revert to a depression he had not experienced for years. Ian came to the Uplift (as Susan did later) and began putting Uplift principles to work both with his partner and all four kids. Age-appropriate rules and consequences were drawn up and posted on the fridge. Susan and Ian began presenting a united front and exchanging needs regularly. They declared their bedroom a no-go zone and set aside one night a week for their "romance evening," which nothing short of a medical emergency was allowed to interfere with. The structure seemed to reassure the kids, who began to accept the new situation as a lasting one and stopped many of their efforts to sabotage it.

If you're contemplating creating a blended family, be sure to discuss your plans with the children and give them some time to adjust to the idea first. However, don't expect young children to be happy at the prospect. They fear the loss of their biological parent's attention and a diminution of their own importance and see the new marriage as the final failure of their efforts to reunite their original family. Many children will develop disruptive and destructive behaviors aimed (usually unconsciously) at separating you and your new partner and thus reuniting you with their father or mother.

Don't kid yourself that loving your new charges just as much as your own children will be easy or happen overnight. Our very genes are against us in that regard, and you'll have to be vigilant to remain fair. The combination of our instinctive desire to protect those genetically ours and children's resentment of "interloping" stepparents can be a powerful brew indeed, and not everyone succeeds. Stepparents—of both sexes—have been shown to pay less attention to their stepchildren's health, safety, and even food requirements according to research by Anne Case and Christina Paxson, professors at Princeton University.[6] Studies also show that stepchildren are more liable to be abused by stepparents than biological parents.

Here are some guidelines to help stepparents:

- Don't show favoritism, if you can possibly help it, because it will make your partner's children feel rejected. Remember, they probably already feel abandoned both by the parent they're not living with as well as the one who is remarrying.

- Hold frequent Family Powwows to begin to create a unified and functional family. You may encounter significant resistance, but hold the powwows anyway, letting children know that this is their opportunity to have a say in rules and family decisions.

- Create new traditions and rituals, building on those the children are already familiar with from their previous families and adding to them. Use the Family Mission Statement to identify unique values and characteristics of your new family.

- When possible, make sure that the children have the opportunity to spend time with their other biological parents (assuming they aren't abusive).

- Don't push your joint children into being great pals, as they will just resist even more. Give them time to get used to the situation and each other in their own ways.

- Don't expect your stepchildren to call you Mom or Dad. Mom and Dad may always be their biological parents, or they may come to use those terms when referring to you.

- Set aside some time each day to connect one-on-one with each child and stepchild.

- Don't attempt to do it all alone. Make sure that you get outside information and support. A good place to start is the Stepfamily Association of America (saafamilies.org).

SINGLE PARENTS LIVING ALONE

More of us, particularly mothers, are finding ourselves faced with the enormous challenge of bringing up a child solo. When we were signing copies of *Creating Optimism* at a store in Tallahassee, Florida, the manager, a single mom, pleaded for us to include advice for single parents in our next book, and she isn't the only one to do so. According to a 1998 Census Bureau report, more than 23 percent of all children live with a lone mother and 4.4 percent with a lone father.[7]

Many, if not all, solitary single parents we've talked to report feeling isolated and unsupported. It's hard to find good-paying work with flexible hours and even harder to find good, affordable child care. But the greatest problem is surrounding yourself and your child with the all-important nexus of supportive relationships. Identifying and going against your negative relationship patterns (perhaps with the help of a therapist), writing Needs Lists for existing and potential relationships, making sure you build socializing as a routine into your life, and looking for organizations that offer support and events for both you and your child, such as Parents Without Partners (parentswithoutpartners.org), are all essential—even though you may be tempted just to hole up with your child in front of the TV during those few hours when you aren't working or driving her to where she needs to go.

Children of single parents tend to feel particularly frightened of abandonment—usually because the other parent has left, but also because their survival seems to depend on only one person. Any of the techniques already discussed for deepening the relationship with your child, such as involving yourself in her interests and taking her into the decision-making process as soon as she can speak, will help.

Investigate shared housing, ideally with a friend or another single parent. Although some singles feel that having their own place symbolizes success and independence, living alone is not as good as with caring, supportive roommates to help create a stable family environment. If you can't share with a friend, make sure you thoroughly interview as many prospective people as possible, and, if they have children, pay attention to how they get on with yours. Avoid sharing with people who have a history of depressive illness or abusive relationships. One of the best places to get advice and sharing prospects is from the Co-abode organization (co-abode.org).

In addition to using the tips in Chapter 15 for dealing with an ex-partner and helping your child overcome loss, here are some more ideas that single parents have found helpful:

- If you are a woman, find a good male role model (and vice versa for a man). Studies show that access to a father figure aids a child's cognitive development as well as mood.[8] If you don't have friends or other family members to fill the role, check out the Big Brothers Big Sisters movement (bbbsa.org). There are more than five hundred agencies of this organization throughout the United States and many overseas.

- Avoid bringing boyfriends or girlfriends home unless you are in a committed relationship and have worked out together how you are going to explain your relationship to your child. Being introduced to a series of transient lovers can have a profound negative effect on a young child.

- Make *consistent* child care arrangements with a person or facility you trust (see Chapter 17 for advice on choosing child care).

- Maintain a balanced optimism. Look for positive things to say about life, and never let your child feel that you think your situation is hopeless. Remember, she will be trying to read your moods and taking her cues from you. Share problems with a confidant and/or therapist, rather than putting your child in that role.

MULTIGENERATIONAL FAMILIES

If you have a good relationship with one or both parents, consider living with them. Studies by Professors Ariel Kalil and Thomas DeLeire of the University of Chicago have shown that children do better in multigenerational families than with sole or cohabiting parents. For a child, a mother/grandparent arrangement can be as good as—and sometimes superior to—a conventional marriage,[9] depending on the parental skills of the grandparent.[10]

However, just because she's your mother doesn't mean that she's always right (or wrong!) and that you don't need to work on the relationship and establish boundaries. In fact, you may find yourself falling back into childhood patterns and fighting old battles—only now, with your child at issue. No matter how odd it feels to be doing this with your own parent, insist on exchanging Needs Lists, agreeing on house rules, and holding Family Powwows to sort out problems. Ultimately, however, it's your child and your responsibility to make sure her needs are met.

> **Tip:** Without blaming your mother (or father) for mistakes you believe she made with you, discuss how your parenting style may be different from hers and how you want her to help parent your child.

COHABITING FAMILIES

Statistically, cohabiting arrangements are far less secure than conventional marriages, but this instability, which can be so damaging to children, shows up mostly in couples who have experienced previous failed relationships and have no plans to marry.[11]

If you are cohabiting, think of what your partner would need to do—or not do—to make you and your child feel secure in the relationship. What specific actions would demonstrate long-term commitment? Marriage as a legal entity may not mean very much to either of you, but the ritual itself is a time-honored pledge that you will stay together "for better or worse, for richer or poorer, in sickness and in health." Many nontraditional couples create commitment ceremonies that formalize their union in their own eyes as well as the eyes of their friends and, perhaps most important, their child.

In fact, nontraditional families need rituals even more than traditional ones to emphasize their durability and give children a sense of security. Here is where the Family Powwow and Family Mission Statement also take on new meaning. What does your family stand for, and what are its rules and mores?

Often, cohabiting couples find that they've moved in together without any agreement about what they want for the future, causing insecurity, conflict, and arguments. In addition to making and exchanging the all-important Needs Lists, discuss and come to agreement on what you both want from the future. Talk about long-term plans, from holidays to careers, and make sure your child hears you doing so and, if old enough, joins in the discussion.

Isolation is another danger to avoid. According to Professor Jan E. Stets of University of California, Riverside, many cohabiting couples cut themselves off, especially from neighbors and family, and often become more isolated than either single moms or married couples, leading to major problems both for the partners and children.[12]

One reason members of cohabiting couples feel insecure is lack of common possessions or assets. Budgeting as a couple and owning joint savings accounts, mutual funds, or property can help give a sense of permanence to the relationship and safety to your child. The aim of a secure, well-bonded family is functional interdependence in which each party's needs are met and boundaries are clear, rather than individualism. Perhaps sharing finances is a need you have of your partner. Or, if you don't trust your partner enough to share finances, let her know what she would need to do to gain your trust.

Whatever your situation, you can use the tools we've outlined in this chapter and others to make it as secure—and thus depression-proof—for your child as possible. Just remember, the more caring and supportive people you can involve in raising your child, the better.

17

MONITORING OUTSIDE INFLUENCES

☉

No matter how good your parenting skills and your relationship with your partner, you cannot entirely insulate your child from society. Nor should you. If you've attended to the important things with him and each other during his first six years, you've laid the groundwork for his later safety and well-being.

Within those first six years, however, you need to protect him as much as possible from the worst aspects of society's dysfunction while preparing him to ultimately make his own choices. It is your task to limit the corrupting influences whose interests lie in making him depressed, anxious, fearful, isolated, and consumer-driven, forces so damaging they constitute emotional, cognitive, and even physical abuse.

The most influential of these, and the most potentially harmful, come from four main areas: media, especially television, the Internet, and video games; advertising and sponsorship messages; bullies and other dysfunctional playmates; and child caregivers such as nannies, kindergarten and preschool teachers, and child care workers, some of whom may be abusive or simply unskilled.

Of course, not everything that comes in from the outside is bad—there are good TV programs, marvelous educational websites, and warm, caring, and professional child minders and kindergartens. Some parents try to totally isolate their children—discouraging them from having playmates or from socializing or cutting them off from all media—and this is bad parenting. But in these early years, you and your partner are the censors, the gatekeepers, and the role models for functional interaction with society.

MEDIA: THE GOOD, THE BAD, AND THE UGLY

"If you don't let me play *Nukem*, I'll kill you! Bitch!"

Five-year-old Andrew was talking to his mother, and he was serious. He had been given this video game by his divorced father and they'd been playing it, and other games such as *Mortal Kombat*, together during the boy's court-ordered visits to his father's house. The outburst was by no means the only example of Andrew's defiant behavior and aggression toward his mother.

Of course television, games, and the Internet are not entirely bad. They can, and do, serve a useful purpose in providing education, information, and harmless entertainment. But for every "Sesame Street" there are a dozen dysfunctional daytime soaps; bad-taste game and reality shows; newscasts with shocking, disturbing, and violent images; and literally hundreds of ads for junk food, toys, and clothing. For every educational video game there are many easily available and extremely violent ones.

According to researchers, including Kansas State University psychology professor John Murray, media violence promotes aggression, desensitization, a lack of empathy, greater propensity to harm others, and a fearful worldview.[1] Video images affect children in this way because they impact the same areas of the brain that cause anxiety, depression, and posttraumatic stress disorder (PTSD), explains Murray.

Other researchers, such as Professor Craig Anderson of Iowa State University, link video games and television to a wide range of antisocial behaviors in young children (particularly boys), which cause them to be diagnosed with "conduct disorder" or "oppositional defiant disorder."[2]

Fortunately, there are things you can do to greatly mitigate the problem of harmful media influences.

- Carefully monitor what your young child watches on TV or the Web. Research shows that children whose exposure to video violence has been subsequently reduced become markedly less disruptive and aggressive.[3]

- Use the Family Powwow to decide what programs, games, and websites will be allowed into your house.

- Limit your young child's TV watching to one hour a day.

- Discuss with your child the violence he sees and its real-life consequences, including ways to solve problems without violence.

TERRORISM AND TRAUMATIC EVENTS

Thanks largely to the media, images and news of disaster, war, and terrorism are delivered directly to our living rooms and, as a result, also to our school-yards and playgrounds. Even very young children absorb more than we might think and can become confused, fearful for their own safety, and possibly suffer PTSD.[4] While it's important to limit their direct exposure to fright-ening images, there are additional ways you can help them come to terms with terrible events.

You can't hide your reaction to horrible events, and even your very young child will pick up on your emotions. It's important to reassure him that he's not the cause of your sadness or anger. If he persists in asking why you are sad, you can say that some people got hurt, but emphasize that your family is safe. If your three- to five-year-old has heard about bad events, talk about them in concrete terms, again stressing his safety.

For example, if you were trying to explain the terrorist attack of Septem-ber 11, 2001, you might say something like: "A very sad, scary thing hap-pened. Some really nasty people blew up buildings in New York and Washington. A lot of people were hurt and some of them died. We're safe. No one is trying to get us. But we are sad and angry that this happened to other people." You might follow this with: "People in lots of countries are try-ing to make sure this doesn't happen again." Don't be afraid to include value statements, such as: "The people who did this were bad. Killing people is never a good way to solve problems."

During a crisis, it's important to try to keep your life as normal as possible. Young kids can recover from almost any distressing external event if they see that their lives have not been affected and their routine is not disturbed. Their resilience will increase if you give them extra hugs or spend more time with them. Allow them to talk about the events; listen to what they say their friends are telling them. Point out where you think they're wrong or where they're exaggerating.

It's normal for children to regress when they're scared. During the weeks after any disaster, your child may be more clingy than usual, wet his bed, and have trouble going to sleep. It's important not to get angry or punish him for these behaviors—that will only confirm his magical thinking that he's responsible for your anger and perhaps even for the events themselves.

Tip: While your child is awake, try to get your news from non-TV sources such as the radio, newspaper, or Web.

SPONSORSHIP AND ADVERTISING

Parents are in grave danger of having their influence and authority usurped by carefully crafted commercial messages that vie for control of their children's minds, starting very early. Even many ten-year-olds don't understand the purpose of advertising or the difference between the content of a show and the commercials around it.[5] Certainly no six-year-old would. To them, it's just an authority figure telling them what to do—no more or less persuasive than any other adult (including you).

Of course, preschoolers and toddlers may not remember brand names, even after multiple exposures to them, but they do remember scenes from the commercials[6] and take on board the underlying metamessage—that there is something innately good and virtuous about the act of purchasing and that it is essential to gaining friends and self-esteem.

The products most advertised to young children are foodstuffs. Professor Mary Story of the University of Minnesota says: "Multiple techniques and

channels are used to reach youth, beginning when they are toddlers, to foster brand-building and influence food product purchase behavior. These food
marketing channels include television advertising, in-school marketing, product placements, kids clubs, the Internet, toys and products with brand logos,
and youth-targeted promotions, such as cross-selling and tie-ins. Foods marketed to children are predominantly high in sugar and fat, and as such are
inconsistent with national dietary recommendations."[7]

People regularly seen on the media become, in a sense, part of the family and act as powerful role models. A study by Professor Sharon Lennon of
Ohio State University showed that even adults make "pseudorelationships"
with pitch people on TV, which leads them to make impulse purchases.[8] This
pseudo-relationship-forming mechanism is even truer of young children. In
fact, children as young as twelve months old are swayed by what adults on
television seem to prefer or reject.[9]

Here's what you can do:

- Keep the TV tuned to PBS or other noncommercial TV outlets when
  your kids are watching.

- Watch TV with your child. Research has shown that a child is more
  susceptible to advertising if she is watching TV alone and that she is
  less likely to demand the things that she sees touted if you are
  watching with her.[10]

- As part of your Family Mission Statement, develop a value system that
  you and your partner live by that is nonmaterialistic. Talk to your
  preschooler about the harm that consumerism can do.

- Explain to your child that what advertisers say or imply in their
  messages is not necessarily the truth.

- Show your child by your example that you are more interested in
  pursuing "value happiness" than instant gratification.

- Do not use the TV or a computer as a substitute nanny.

BULLIES AND VICTIMS

Our violence-prone society is reflected in the microcosm of the home and schoolyard, where bullying and ostracism are increasing problems and can lead to depression. Numerous studies have shown that bullying is largely learned at home, day care, and school through a failure of regulation.[11] So is victimhood—the behavioral characteristics that indicate to a bully which classmate, teammate, or playmate is a potential target.[12]

Contrary to popular belief, not all bullies are taking out their low self-esteem on weaker children; many have simply been taught to get their needs met through aggression. Some researchers, including Professor David Wolke of the University of Hertfordshire in England, have found that the majority of bullies (who are not themselves victims) were physically and emotionally healthier than their victims,[13] and several studies show that they have high self-esteem.[14]

Bullies are usually very well aware that what they are doing is morally wrong, but experience has taught them that they can get away with it. Preschool children tend to be altruistic and prosocial when there is an adult present and decidedly less so when there is not. In biological terms, this is quite understandable. As with chicks in a nest, rewards, and thus survival chances, tend to go to the strongest. In times of scarcity, this aggression—what we call bullying—can be a sensible strategy.[15]

And, of course, we do live in a time of scarcity—not lack of food necessarily, but of attention, time, and attachment. A stronger sibling will bully a weaker one to gain dominance and thus access to emotional sustenance. The same will happen in any crowded classroom, kindergarten, competitive office environment, or home in which the parents, teachers, or other adult authority figures have insufficient time to devote to their charges.

Primary school children share three attitudes to bullying: great admiration for the bullies, a tendency to despise the victims, and an avowed support for the idea that an adult should intervene on the victim's behalf.[16] Generally, bullies are more outgoing and extroverted and often more popular than their victims, who are typically loners with fewer social skills.[17] Some of this social approval comes from the fact that the bully is only doing to the less popular kid what the other children would like to do.

Who, then, is a bully? It's not all that clear-cut. Some children are always the bullies and some are the perpetual victims. However, most bullies are also, at times, victims. A boy might bully his sister or playmates yet, at the same time, live in fear of an authoritarian parent or be bullied by his older brother or other children.[18]

What's more, bullying is often seen differently from the points of view of the victim, parents, or teachers.[19] Six-year-old Joseph, who had started first grade in a school in a rough neighborhood, did not tell his parents that bullying was a recess rite of passage. His parents had always regarded his boisterous roughhousing with his younger brother Isaac as a benign expression of boyishness and ignored the bruising that began to appear on Isaac's arms, legs, and trunk, thinking that, since he didn't complain, all must be well. They did, however, notice that the younger sibling was becoming more listless and seemed to have less interest in things he once found enjoyable. When they asked what was wrong, his usual answer was "nothing" or "I'm OK." One day his father found Isaac crying in his room. When he asked what the matter was, Isaac said, "I can't tell. Joe will beat me up." What seemed harmless play to his parents was to Isaac intolerable bullying.

Some bullies and almost all bully/victims and victims are more depressed than their peers. In fact, they are all potential suicide risks as adolescents, according to a major study reported in the *British Medical Journal*.[20] While pure bullies have usually not themselves been targets, most bullies share a troubled or neglectful home life and come from households where there is a lot of parental fighting, physical or verbal. Bully/victims are generally the victims of family violence (including corporal punishment) or threats.[21]

Victims often come from families with secrets, where there is a culture of silence and social isolation, which may make them more vulnerable by preventing them from reporting bullying and seeking adult help. They tend to be shorter than their peers and a large percentage of them have been victims of sibling bullying.[22]

John Pearce, professor of Child and Adolescent Psychiatry at Nottingham University, lists a number of emotional characteristics that define a victim: anxious temperament, low self-esteem, insecurity, lack of friends, emotional reactivity, easily dominated, and nonaggressive.

ANTIBULLYING STRATEGIES

You can't just expect your child to grow out of being a bully or a victim. Once it's ingrained, it stays.[23] Following the strategies below throughout the toddler and preschool years will ensure that your child does not become either.

- Avoid fighting or being aggressive toward each other. Children pick up aggression as a means of problem-solving. Use the Family Powwow and Needs-Based Dialogue to solve problems.

- Teach your child that aggression is unacceptable as a means of getting his needs met. Clearly identify the behaviors you find objectionable and establish specific rules and consequences.

- Don't use corporal punishment. There is never a good reason to hit a child and doing so leads to depression and aggressive behavior.

- Don't play favorites. Give equal time and attention to all your children.

- Don't keep secrets or ask your child to keep secrets.

- If a child complains of being bullied inside or outside the home, take it seriously and do something about it.

- Teach your child to make his needs known and establish appropriate boundaries. Bullies rarely pick on those who are aware of and firmly communicate their own boundaries.

- Make sure that any rewards the bully has gotten from his actions are immediately confiscated. Find some way in which he can "repay" his victim. An apology is a good start.

- Remember that most instances of bullying by a family member indicate an underlying problem of the family as a whole. It is time to reassess family rules, boundaries, and relationships.

CHOOSING APPROPRIATE CHILD CARE

Child care is one of the most controversial issues of our time. In our view, institutional child care before the age of twelve months is potentially harmful, and even full-time day care may not be a good idea before preschool. Yet the economic facts of life often dictate that some sort of child care is the only option.

The advocates of institutionalized child care, such as Joan Peters in her 1998 book *When Mothers Work: Loving Our Children Without Sacrificing Ourselves*,[24] argue that children in child care develop faster and in the end become more successful in school and in later life. Their opponents, such as Mary Eberstadt, author of the best-selling *Home-Alone America*, dispute this. Eberstadt sees depression and other psychiatric problems, antisocial behavior, drug-taking, crime, and unsafe sex as the results of America's experiment with nonmaternal day care.[25] About the only thing both sides agree on is that bad child care, of whatever kind, is extremely harmful psychologically and physically.

In order to mitigate the harmful effects of early separation, you need to carefully prepare your child for the experience of day care and be sure to choose the right kind of child care, institution, or minder. There's a bewildering amount of advice about the best type of care, much of it put out by the child care industry itself or individual child care facilities. There are also a wide range of child care arrangements, including nannies, crèches, play schools, playgroups, institutionalized child care facilities, part- or full-time child minders, home-based child care, mother and baby groups, cooperative minding, and, of course, baby-sitters.

Before you set out to find the right arrangement, work out exactly what you need the child care to allow you to do: go to work part-time, go to work full-time, take occasional "time-outs," or do daily or weekly shopping. Some kinds of child care are more flexible than others. Don't mix and match child care arrangements haphazardly. Young children derive their sense of safety from routine: doing the same thing with the same people at the same time each day.

Family Care

In most cases, the best child minders are family members, including your partner, mother, mother-in-law, and older children. However, there are instances in which a family member might not be the right choice. Nadia, who had spend many years overcoming her mother's harsh criticism and physical punishment, felt she still owed it to her daughter to make sure she spent time with her grandma. When it was pointed out that she was simply setting her daughter up to suffer the same legacy, Nadia changed her mind and made other child care arrangements. Although she still felt twinges of guilt about excluding her own parent, she realized she was doing the best for her daughter.

Similarly, be careful about leaving your young child in the care of a very jealous or unwilling sibling, who might consciously or unconsciously take out his frustrations on his little brother or sister.

Nannies and Baby-Sitters

If you're going to work full-time and there is no trusted family member available, a good nanny is undoubtedly the best option. It is, however, probably the most costly and the most complex in terms of paperwork and taxes. As your child's surrogate mother, a nanny should be brought in early so that your child can form a secure attachment to her and ideally would be there at least until your child goes to kindergarten.

In addition to obvious advice such as checking references, giving detailed information of your requirements to a reputable recruitment agency, and agreeing on a trial period, draw on the relationship techniques we've discussed so far to select the best person.

Draw up a detailed job description for the role, including such things as whether you want her to help with laundry and prepare the child's meals; whether it's OK for her to look after her own children in addition to yours at your house; and whether she needs to drive and thus must have a license.

Create a Needs List that has to do with the relationship you want to have with her and her to have with your child. Many of your needs (and guidelines for an interview) will also apply to baby-sitters. Examples are: "I need you to tell the truth," "I need you to do what you say you will," or, "I need you to praise him at least five times a day and never criticize." If you're looking for a live-in nanny, think of needs you'd have of someone who'll be sharing your home, such as "I need you to say good morning and smile in the mornings" and "If you are upset, I need you to tell us if it has to do with us and, if so, what you need us to do differently."

Discuss your needs at the interview, and be sure to ask what she would need from you, in concrete and actionable terms, to make the experience and the relationships a success. During the discussion, also assess her skills at relationships and her child-rearing philosophy. Remember that this person will have to bond with your child and may be an essential part of his growing up. Don't be afraid to ask questions about her childhood (remember that we tend to re-create the past). You should probably hold several discussions with suitable nanny applicants, and she should meet your partner (and, of course, your child) as well. Questions could include:

- How long did you stay with your last employer, and how long do you plan to stay here?

- What did you like or dislike about where you were last? (Her answer may indicate the value she places on relationships and her ability to form them.)

- How were you disciplined as a child, and by whom? (You're looking for an experience of appropriate boundary setting and consequences. If her parents used physical punishment, you should be concerned and dig deeper. Does she realize that this was wrong?)

- Who praised you when you were little, and for what?

- How did your parents get along with each other and the kids?

- If you could change one thing about your early childhood, what would it be?

An applicant's body language is very telling. A rigid posture may suggest anxiety that could be passed on to your child; rounded, stooped shoulders indicate that she's been criticized and may be critical; and one shoulder higher than the other may be an echo of physical abuse. The more at ease she is with her own body, the more likely she is to have an appropriate and affectionate physical connection with your child. Does she offer your child the opportunity for physical contact rather than rush or avoid it? Trust your gut (stomach brain) about how well your child seems to be getting on with each candidate.

External Child Care

Institutional care is likely to be highly stressful for your child. Researchers led by Lieselotte Ahnert of the Free University of Berlin found that levels of the stress hormone cortisol have been shown to rise up to 100 percent above normal levels when U.S. children of fifteen months are put into child care.[26] If these levels of stress are continued over an extended period of time, depression and anxiety are the inevitable result.

You can make the transition easier in several ways. Stay with your child the first few times so that he can get used to the surroundings in a nonthreatening way. Allow him to take his favorite toy. If he's old enough, prepare him by talking about the experience and about the new friends he will meet. Encourage him to voice his fears and anxieties about being apart from you.

Before choosing a facility, ask yourself whether you want a situation that emphasizes play or learning, and check out a number of alternatives, preferably with your child. Observe what goes on for at least two hours, and make notes so that you and your partner can discuss all the options. At each place:

- Ask about the number of children and adult-child ratio. There should be about one adult for every four children.

- Watch how caregivers interact with the children. Do they seem supportive and friendly? Do they reinforce social behavior among children? Are children gently encouraged to try new activities? Do caretakers seem flexible, confident, competent, and sensitive? Do the children seem happy? How does the staff handle accidents, fighting, emotional upsets, and sleepiness?

- Inspect carefully the facility's appearance. Is it clean, cheerful, safe, and light (very important in preventing depression)? Is there a quiet area? Is there a well-equipped playground for toddlers and older children (essential for avoiding ADD/ADHD)?

- Ask about the values and beliefs of those who run the center, including the director's (or caretaker's) personal child care philosophy.

- Watch how the children play. Do the toys encourage both large and fine motor development? Are there materials for dramatic play, artwork, and solitary play? Are children gently encouraged to "have a go," or are they pressured?

- Notice how the caregiver or center management interacts with parents. Do you feel that your needs are respected or that parents are just inconveniences who happen to pay the bills? Can parents drop in unannounced to be with their kids? Do they have regular parent-caretaker conferences? Can parents make suggestions about the center or how to interact with their children? Can you be flexible with the hours your child is there?

- Notice how happy your child seems at each location.

Monitoring outside influences on your child within a dysfunctional society will never be easy, and no one can do it flawlessly. Here is where you and your partner may need to review and even further develop your values, find common ground, and strongly support and encourage each other. While the task is serious, never forget that the final goal is a happy household full of love and cheer—not a perfect one.

CONCLUSION

⊙

Good, optimistic parenting is not a simple or easy skill, particularly in our dysfunctional society. The guidance we've provided will help you to raise an optimistic, resilient child who can learn the skills she needs to face the challenges she meets and, even more important, surround herself with supportive, loving people to help her.

However, all this information may seem a bit overwhelming at first, especially if you feel you need to do things perfectly. You will probably want to refer back to certain chapters and share points of interest, if not the whole book, with your partner and others who are involved in your child's care. Above all, keep in mind the following secrets of optimistic families.

• **Good relationships within the family.** How you and your partner (or other caregivers) support each other is perhaps the biggest factor in both your well-being and that of your child. Yet it can be frighteningly easy to take these relationships for granted in the throes of hectic work schedules and caring for a young child. Watch for the danger signs we've outlined, such as letting family rituals slip or falling back into bad habits such as criticism and not spending not enough time together. Think about and clearly identify your needs to all family members, people involved in your child's care, and even friends and colleagues.

• **Time and attention.** In our modern society, these are often the scarcest commodities. Prioritize carefully, with emphasis on what's really important to you both, and stick to your plans. Remember that the first six years are by far the most formative, and the first twenty months, in particular, will determine the strength of the bond your child forms with you. Time spent with her now will pay immeasurable lifelong dividends. Plenty of appropriate praise and acknowledgment will build self-esteem and competence and eventually enable her to pass on the culture of praise to her own family.

- **Empathy and consistency.** Demonstrating these all-important parenting qualities can be difficult at first, especially if your parents weren't sure how to be empathic and consistent with you. However, these qualities can be learned. Think about what your child might be feeling or needing, and through your interest and questions as she gets older, teach her to express her emotions and needs to you. Work with your partner and the whole family to establish a consistent routine and clear and constant boundaries.

- **Shared family values.** Take a cue from our hunter-gatherer ancestors and modern researchers, and draw on the strong bonding power of joint values, beliefs, spirituality, and rituals. Talk to your child about what matters to you, and as she gets older, ask her opinion (remember the Family Mission Statement). Positive family values, such as striving for authentic, long-term happiness versus short-term gain, and appreciating good relationships, serve as a buffer against the barrage of negative messages of our conflict-ridden and consumerist society.

- **A challenging natural environment.** Nature is your savior as well as your child's. Regular play and exercise in a natural environment is vital to physical and emotional health. What's more, it gives your child a chance to be a child, which is becoming increasingly rare in our society. Experience the joy of unfettered activities, challenging surfaces that stimulate movement skills, and the sounds, scents, and sights that nurture us at the deepest levels.

In order to claim our birthright of optimism, we need simply to be human, to create the conditions under which humans were meant to live: loving, supportive relationships, access to the natural world, and beliefs that inspire and connect us. Under these conditions, your child—and you—can look forward to an optimistic, healthy, and fulfilling life.

ENDNOTES

⊙

INTRODUCTION

1. J. Najman, et al., "Predictors of Depression in Very Young Children: A Prospective Study," *Social Psychiatry and Psychiatric Epidemiology* 40, no. 5 (2005): 367–74.

CHAPTER 1

1. Rachel Yehuda, et al., "Transgenerational Effects of Posttraumatic Stress Disorder in Babies of Mothers Exposed to the World Trade Center Attacks During Pregnancy," *Journal of Clinical Endocrinology and Metabolism*, 3 May 2005, doi:10.1210/jc.2005-0550.
2. Thomas Delate, et al., "Trends in the Use of Antidepressants in a National Sample of Commercially Insured Pediatric Patients, 1998 to 2002," *Psychiatric Services* 55, no. 4 (2004): 387–91.
3. M. L. Murray, et al., "A Drug Utilisation Study of Antidepressants in Children and Adolescents Using the General Practice Research Database," *Archives of Disease in Childhood* 89, no. 12 (2004): 1098–102.
4. C. Adams and A. Young, "Giving Antidepressants to Children May Not Work, FDA Says," *Knight Ridder Newspapers*, 15 February 2004.
5. Association of American Colleges and Universities, "Bringing Theory to Practice: Depression, Substance Abuse, and College Student Engagement," July 2004 report quoted by Kevin Bergquist in "Engaging a New

Way of Battling Substance Abuse and Depression," *The University Record*, University of Michigan, 6 July 2004.

6. Ronald C. Kessler, et al., "Lifetime Prevalence and Age-of-Onset Distributions of DSM-IV Disorders in the National Comorbidity Survey Replication," *Archives of General Psychiatry* 62, no. 6 (2005): 593–602.

7. William Kanapaux, "The Patient as Parent: Family Matters," *Psychiatric Times* 19, no. 10 (2002).

8. W. R. Beardslee, et al., "Children of Affectively Ill Parents: A Review of the Past 10 Years," *Journal of the American Academy of Child and Adolescent Psychiatry* 37, no. 11 (1998): 1134–41.

9. Bjørn Grinde, *Darwinian Happiness: Evolution as a Guide for Living and Understanding Human Behavior* (Princeton, NJ: Darwin Press, 2002).

10. Robert Wright, "Evolution of Despair," *Time*, 28 August 1995; also M. Brewer, "Taking the Social Origins of Human Nature Seriously," *Personality and Social Psychology Review* 8, no. 2 (2004): 107–13.

11. Bjørn Grinde, 2002.

12. Matt Ridley, *Nature via Nurture: Genes, Experience and What Makes Us Human* (New York: HarperCollins, 2003).

13. Sarah Stewart-Brown and R. Shaw, "Relationships in the Home and Health in Later Life: The Roots of Social Capital," in *Social Capital for Health* (London: Health Development Agency, 2004).

14. M. J. Cox, et al., "Marriage, Adult Adjustment, and Early Parenting," *Child Development* 60, no. 5 (1989): 1015–24.

15. Wyndol Furman and Anna Smalley Flanagan, "The Influence of Earlier Relationships on Marriage: An Attachment Perspective," in *Clinical Handbook of Marriage and Couples Intervention*, ed. W. K. Halford and H. J. Markman (Chichester, UK: Wiley, 1996).

16. Deborah Lott, "Brain Development, Attachment and Impact on Psychic Vulnerability," *Psychiatric Times* 15, no. 5 (1998): 1–5.

17. Vicky Flory, "A Novel Clinical Intervention for Severe Childhood Depression and Anxiety," *Clinical Child Psychology and Psychiatry* 9, no. 1 (2004): 9–23.

18. Daniel J. Siegel, "Cognitive Neuroscience Encounters Psychotherapy: Lessons from Research on Attachment and the Development of Emotion, Memory and Narrative," *Psychiatric Times* 13, no. 3 (1996).

19. Froma Walsh, *Strengthening Family Resilience* (New York: Guilford Press, 1998), 45.
20. Nancy M. Wells, "At Home with Nature: Effects of 'Greenness' on Children's Cognitive Functioning," *Environment and Behavior* 32, no. 6 (2000): 775–95.

CHAPTER 2

1. Allan N. Schore, quoted by Deborah Lott in "Brain Development, Attachment and Impact on Psychic Vulnerability," *Psychiatric Times* 15 (1998): 5.
2. Allan N. Schore, "The Neurobiology of Attachment and Early Personality Organization," *Journal of Prenatal and Perinatal Psychology and Health* 16, no. 3 (2002): 249–63.
3. Ibid.
4. Robert Karen, *Becoming Attached: First Relationships and How They Shape Our Capacity to Love* (New York: Oxford University Press, 1998).
5. P. Leach, "Infant Care from Infants' Viewpoint: The Views of Some Professionals," *Early Development and Parenting* 6, no. 2 (1998): 47–58.
6. Kyle D. Pruett, "Role of the Father," *Pediatrics* 102, no. 5 (1998): 1253–61.
7. M. Iacoboni, et al., "Cortical Mechanisms of Human Imitation," *Science* 286, no. 5449 (1999): 2526–28.
8. Allan Schore, 2002.
9. Elizabeth Mezzacappa, "A Preliminary Analysis of the Association between Breast-Feeding and Depressive Symptomology," paper presented at the American Psychosomatic Society Annual Meeting, 15 March 2002, Barcelona.
10. W. Sears, et al., *The Baby Book*, 2d ed. (New York: Little Brown, 2003).
11. Ibid.
12. James Herzog, "Birth to Two," Sesame Street Parents, sesameworkshop.org/parents/advice/article.php?contentId=630&#1.
13. Ibid.

14. J. E. Cox and W. G. Bithoney, "Fathers of Children Born to Adolescent Mothers: Predictors of Contact with Their Children at 2 Years," *Archives of Pediatric Adolescent Medicine* 149, no. 9 (1995): 962–66.

15. J. Belsky, "Mother-Father-Infant Interaction: A Naturalistic Observational Study," *Developmental Psychology* 15 (1979): 601–7.

16. J. K. Nugent, "Cultural and Psychological Influences on the Father's Role in Infant Development," *Journal of Marriage and the Family* 53, no. 2 (1991): 475–85.

17. L. J. Cohen and J. J. Campos, "Father, Mother, and Stranger as Elicitors of Attachment Behaviors in Infancy," *Developmental Psychology* 10, no. 1 (1974): 146–54.

18. James Herzog.

CHAPTER 3

1. Steven Dubovsky, *Mind-Body Deceptions: The Psychomatics of Everyday Life* (New York: Norton & Co., 1997).

2. Ronald C. Kessler, et al., "Posttraumatic Stress Disorder in the National Comorbidity Survey," *Archives of General Psychiatry* 52, no. 12 (1995): 1048–60.

3. J. I. Escobar, et al., "Somatization in the Community," *Archives of General Psychiatry* 44, no. 8 (1987): 713–18.

4. Shaila Misri, et al., "Relation Between Prenatal Maternal Mood and Anxiety and Neonatal Health," *Canadian Journal of Psychiatry* 49, no. 10 (2004): 684–89; Peter W. Nathanielsz, *Life in the Womb: The Origin of Health and Disease* (Ithaca, NY: Promethean Press, 1999).

5. Peter Nathanielsz, 1999.

6. T. Field, "Maternal Depression Effects on Infants and Early Interventions," *Preventive Medicine* 27, no. 2 (1998): 200–203; M. Beeghly, et al., "Specificity of Preventative Pediatric Intervention Effects in Early Infancy," *Journal of Developmental and Behavioral Pediatrics* 16, no. 3 (1995): 158–66.

7. K. A. Espy, et al., "Neuropsychologic Function in Toddlers Exposed to Cocaine in Utero: A Preliminary Study," *Developmental Neuropsychology* 15 (1999): 447–60.

8. Shaila Misri, 2004.

9. E. Hawkins-Walsh, "Turning Primary Care Providers' Attention to Child Behavior: A Review of the Literature," *Journal of Pediatric Health Care* 15, no. 3 (2001): 115–22.

10. Biederman, J., et al., "Psychiatric Comorbidity Among Referred Juveniles with Major Depression: Fact or Artifact?" *Journal of the American Academy of Child Adolescent Psychiatry* 34, no. 5 (1995): 579–90.

11. D. G. Nemeth, C. C. Creveling, et al., "Misdiagnosis of ADHD When Alternative Diagnoses Is Warranted," paper presented at the Belgium meeting of the International Neuropsychological Society, 12–15 July 2000, Brussels.

12. J. L. Luby, et al., "The Clinical Picture of Depression in Preschool Children," *Journal of the American Academy of Child and Adolescent Psychiatry* 42, no. 3 (2003): 340–48.

13. J. Najman, et al., "Predictors of Depression in Very Young Children: A Prospective Study," *Social Psychiatry and Psychiatric Epidemiology* 40, no. 5 (2005): 367–74.

14. Deborah Lott, "Childhood Trauma, CRF Hypersecretion and Depression," *Psychiatric Times* 16, no. 10 (1999); Danya Glaser, "Child Abuse and Neglect and the Brain: A Review," *Journal of Child Psychology and Psychiatry* 41, no. 1 (2000): 97–116.

15. T. Moffitt, et al., "Influence of Life Stress on Depression: Moderation by a Polymorphism in the 5-HTT Gene," *Science* 301, no. 5631 (2003): 386–89.

16. J. Kaufman, et al., "Social Supports Lessen Effects of Maltreatment on Children Vulnerable to Depression," *Proceedings of the National Academy of Science*, November 2004.

17. Peter Nathanielsz, 1999.

18. Steven W. Kairys, et al., "The Psychological Maltreatment of Children— Technical Report," *Pediatrics* 109, no. 4 (2002): e68.

19. R. S. Marvin and R. B. Stewart, "A Family System Framework for the Study of Attachment," in *Attachment Beyond the Preschool Years*, ed. M. Greenberg, et al. (Chicago: University of Chicago Press, 1991); J. Byng-Hall, "Family and Couple Therapy: Toward Greater Security," in *Handbook of Attachment: Theory, Research, and Clinical Applications*, ed. J. Cassidy and P. R. Shaver (New York: Guilford Press, 1999).

20. Lee Salk, *What Every Child Would Like His Parents to Know* (New York: Warner Books, 1973), 30–31; also Judith Viorst, *Necessary Losses: The Loves, Illusions, Dependencies, and Impossible Expectations That All of Us Have to Give Up in Order to Grow* (New York: Fawcett, 1986); and John Bowlby, "Grief and Mourning in Infancy and Early Childhood," paper presented in *Psychoanalytic Study of the Child* (1960), cited in *Personality: Dynamics, Development, and Assessment*, I. Janis, et al. (New York: Harcourt, Brace & World, 1969).

21. John Bowlby, 1960.

22. See Robert Karen, *Becoming Attached: First Relationships and How They Shape Our Capacity to Love* (New York: Oxford University Press, 1998).

23. Ibid.

24. L. A. Stroufe, et al., *Child Development: Its Nature and Course*, 2d ed. (New York: McGraw-Hill, 1992).

25. Daniel Goleman, *Emotional Intelligence: Why It Can Matter More Than IQ* (London: Bloomsbury, 1996).

26. J. Jureidini, et al., "Efficacy and Safety of Antidepressants for Children and Adolescents," *British Medical Journal* 328 (2004): 879–83.

27. C. Adams and A. Young, "Giving Antidepressants to Children May Not Work, FDA Says," *Knight Ridder Newspapers*, 15 February 2004.

28. S. Vedantam, "FDA Links Antidepressants, Youth Suicide Risk," *Washington Post*, 23 February 2004, page A01.

29. N. Damluji and J. Ferguson, "Paradoxical Worsening of Depressive Symptomatology Caused by Antidepressants," *Journal of Clinical Psychopharmacology* 8, no. 5 (1988): 347–49.

30. Robert Lefever, "Addiction to Antidepressants," Promis, 2001, promis.co.uk/?view=other/antidepressants.

31. J. Gordon, et al., "Selective Serotonin Reuptake Inhibitors Directly Signal for Apoptosis in Biopsylike Burkitt Lymphoma Cells," *Blood* 101, no. 8 (2003): 3212–19.

32. W. Meijer, et al., "Association of Risk of Abnormal Bleeding with Degree of Serotonin Reuptake Inhibition by Antidepressants," *Archives of Internal Medicine* 164, no. 21 (2004): 2367–70.

CHAPTER 4

1. Robert Karen, *Becoming Attached: First Relationships and How They Shape Our Capacity to Love* (New York: Oxford University Press, 1998), 357.
2. Wyndol Furman and Anna Smalley Flanagan, "The Influence of Earlier Relationships on Marriage: An Attachment Perspective," in *Clinical Handbook of Marriage and Couples Intervention*, ed. W. K. Halford and H. J. Markman (Chichester, UK: Wiley, 1996).
3. S. Fraiberg, et al., "Ghosts in the Nursery: A Psychoanalytic Approach to the Problems of Impaired Infant-Mother Relationships," *Journal of the American Academy of Child Psychiatry* 14, no. 3 (1975): 387–421.
4. A. Slade, interview with Robert Karen, in *Becoming Attached* (New York: Oxford University Press, 1998), 367.

CHAPTER 5

1. Stacey Tantleff-Dunn, in interview with author, 9 December 2004.
2. Christopher J. Ruhm, "How Well Do Parents with Young Children Combine Work and Family Life?" paper presented at Workforce/Workplace Mismatch? Work, Family, Health and Well-Being Conference, in association with NICHD, 16 June 2003.
3. Belinda Probert, "'Grateful Slaves' or 'Self-Made Women': A Matter of Choice or Policy," *Australian Feminist Studies* 17, no. 37 (2002): 7–17.
4. Robert Karen, *Becoming Attached: First Relationships and How They Shape Our Capacity to Love* (New York: Oxford University Press, 1998), 313–44; L. Ahnert, et al., "Transition to Child Care: Associations with InfantMother Attachment, Infant Negative Emotion, and Cortisol Elevations," *Child Development* 75, no. 3 (2004): 639–50.

5. T. S. Zimmerman et al., "Strategies for Reducing Guilt Among Working Mothers," *Colorado Early Childhood Journal* 3, no. 1 (2001): 12–17.

6. L. J. Harrison and J. A. Ungerer, "Maternal Employment and Infant-Mother Attachment Security at 12 Months Postpartum," *Developmental Psychology* 38, no. 5 (2002): 758–73.

7. J. Belsky and D. Eggebeen, "Early and Extensive Maternal Employment and Young Children's Socioemotional Development: Children of the National Longitudinal Survey of Youth," *Journal of Marriage and the Family* 53, no. 4 (1991): 1083–98; J. Belsky, "Developmental Risks (Still) Associated with Early Child Care," *Journal of Child Psychology and Psychiatry* 42, no. 7 (2001): 845–59; Lise M. Youngblade, "Peer and Teacher Ratings of Third- and Fourth-Grade Children's Social Behavior as a Function of Early Maternal Employment," *Journal of Child Psychology and Psychiatry* 44, no. 4 (2003): 477–88; Lawrence M. Berger, et al., "Maternity Leave, Early Maternal Employment and Child Health and Development in the U.S.," *The Economic Journal* 115, no. 501 (2005): F29–47.

8. Stanley Kurtz, "The Guilt Game," Nationalreview.com, 26 April 2001, quoted by Mary Eberstadt in *Home-Alone America: The Hidden Toll of Day Care, Behavioral Drugs, and Other Parent Substitutes* (New York: Sentinel, 2004).

9. Ronald C. Kessler, et al., "Lifetime Prevalence and Age-of-Onset Distributions of DSM-IV Disorders in the National Comorbidity Survey Replication," *Archives of General Psychiatry* 62, no. 6 (2005): 593–602.

10. W. Sears, et al., *The Baby Book*, 2d ed. (New York: Little Brown, 2003).

11. National Institute of Child Health and Human Development, 2003.

12. L. W. Hoffman and L. M. Youngblade, *Mothers at Work: Effects on Children's Well-Being* (New York: Cambridge University Press, 1999).

13. J. S. Hyde, et al., "Children's Temperament and Behavior Problems Predict Their Employed Mothers' Work Functioning," *Child Development* 75, no. 2 (2004): 580–94.

14. M. Tausig and R. Fenwick, "Unbinding Time: Alternate Work Schedules and Work-life Balance," *Journal of Family and Economic Issues* 22, no. 2 (2001): 101–19.

15. Kristin A. Moore, et al., "Tradeoffs Among Work, Family, Health and Well-Being: A Social-Demographic Perspective," paper presented at Workforce/Workplace Mismatch? Work, Family, Health and Well-Being Conference, in association with NICHD, 16 June 2003.

16. Neala S. Schwartzberg and Rita Scher Dytell, "Dual-Earner Families: The Importance of Work Stress and Family Stress for Psychological Well-Being," *Health Psychology* 1, no. 2 (1996): 211–23.

17. C. Lewis, *A Man's Place in the Home: Fathers and Families in the UK* (London: Joseph Rowntree Foundation, 2000).

18. J. Aldous, et al., "Fathering Over Time: What Makes the Difference?" *Journal of Marriage and the Family* 60, no. 4 (1998): 809–20.

19. C. Cooper, quoted in "House Husbands' Heart Risk," *BBC News Online*, 25 April 2002, http://news.bbc.co.uk/hi/english/health/news id_1950000/1950155.stm.

20. Stacey Tantleff-Dunn, interview.

CHAPTER 6

1. J. Belsky, "The Determinants of Parenting: A Process Model," *Child Development* 55, no. 1 (1984): 83–96; P. Amato, "The Legacy of Parents' Marital Discord: Consequences for Children's Marital Quality," *Journal of Personality and Social Psychology* 81, no. 4 (2001): 627–38; D. C. Renshaw, "Fathering," *Psychiatric Times* 21, no. 11 (2004); B. A. McBride, et al., "Child Characteristics, Parenting Stress, and Parental Involvement: Fathers Versus Mothers," *Journal of Marriage and Family* 64, no. 4 (2002): 998–1011.

2. Bjørn Grinde, *Darwinian Happiness: Evolution as a Guide for Living and Understanding Human Behavior* (Princeton, NJ: Darwin Press, 2002).

3. John Bowlby, *The Making and Breaking of Affectional Bonds* (New York: Routledge, 1979).

4. S. Korchin and G. Ruff, cited in John Bowlby, 1979.

5. John Bowlby, 1979.

6. Matt Ridley, *Origins of Virtue: Human Instincts and the Evolution of Cooperation* (New York: Penguin Viking, 1996).
7. James K. Rilling, et al., "A Neural Basis for Social Cooperation," *Neuron* 35, no. 2 (2002): 395–405.
8. J. M. Patterson, "Understanding Family Resilience," *Journal of Clinical Psychology* 58, no. 3 (2002): 233–46.

CHAPTER 7

1. Colin Turnbull, *The Forest People* (London: Pimlico, 1993).
2. Douglas W. Bird, et al., "Mardu Children's Hunting Strategies in the Western Australian Desert," paper for CHAGS, University of Maine, 2000.
3. Donna L. Mumme and Anne Fernald, "The Infant as Onlooker: Learning from Emotional Reactions Observed in a Television Scenario," *Child Development* 74, no. 1 (2003): 221–37.
4. Irwin P. Levin and Stephanie S. Hart, "Risk Preferences in Young Children: Early Evidence of Individual Differences in Reaction to Potential Gains and Losses," *Journal of Behavioral Decision Making* 16, no. 5 (2003): 397–413.
5. Nancy Marie Garon, "Future Oriented Decision Making in Childhood" (Ph.D. dissertation, Dalhousie University, 2004).
6. Carolyn Willow, et al., "Young Children's Citizenship" (London: Joseph Rowntree Foundation, 2004).
7. R. J. Fetsch and T. S. Zimmerman, "Marriage and Family Consultation with Ranch and Farm Families: An Empirical Family Case Study," *Journal of Marital and Family Therapy* 25, no. 4 (1999): 485–501.

CHAPTER 8

1. A. Knafo, "Authoritarians, the Next Generation: Values and Bullying Among Adolescent Children of Authoritarian Fathers," *Analyses of Social Issues and Public Policy* 3, no. 1 (2003): 199–204.

2. Bjørn Grinde, *Darwinian Happiness: Evolution as a Guide for Living and Understanding Human Behavior* (Princeton, NJ: Darwin Press, 2002), 99.

3. B. F. Skinner, "What's Wrong with Daily Life in the Western World," *American Psychologist* 41, no. 5 (1986): 568–74.

4. James Y. Nazroo, "Exploring Gender Difference in Depression," *Psychiatric Times* 18, no. 3 (2001).

5. James Y. Nazroo, et al., "Gender Differences in the Prevalence of Depression: Artefact, Alternative Disorders, Biology or Roles?" *Sociology of Health and Illness* 20, no. 3 (1998): 312–30.

6. Mark R. Beauchamp, et al., "Role Ambiguity, Role Efficacy, and Role Performance: Multidimensional and Mediational Relationships Within Interdependent Sport Teams," *Group Dynamics: Theory, Research and Practice* 6, no. 3 (2002): 229–42.

7. Elizabeth A. Vandewater, et al., "Predicting Women's Well-Being in Midlife: The Importance of Personality Development and Social Role Involvements," *Journal of Personality and Social Psychology* 72, no. 5 (1997): 1147–60.

8. Stacey Tantleff-Dunn, interview with author, 9 December 2004.

9. Elaine Eaker, study for the American Heart Association reported in "House Husbands' Heart Risk," *BBC News Online*, 24 April 2002.

10. K. Miner-Rubino, et al., "Gender, Social Class, and the Subjective Experience of Aging: Self-Perceived Personality Change from Early Adulthood to Late Midlife," *Personality and Social Psychology Bulletin* 30, no. 12 (2004): 1599–610.

11. S. Robert Moradi, "The Father-Child Connection: A Struggle of Contemporary Man," *Psychiatric Times* 14, no. 1 (1997).

12. Ibid.

13. David E. Cortesi, *Secular Wholeness: A Skeptic's Path to a Richer Life* (New Bern, NC: Trafford, 2002), 62.

14. Barbara H. Fiese, et al., "A Review of 50 Years of Research on Naturally Occurring Family Routines and Rituals: Cause for Celebration?" *Journal of Family Psychology* 16, no. 4 (2002): 381–90.

15. Jill Kimball, et al., *Drawing Families Together One Meal at a Time* (Orlando, FL: Active Media Pub, 2003).

CHAPTER 9

1. Roy F. Baumeister, et al., "Does High Self-Esteem Cause Better Performance, Interpersonal Success, Happiness, or Healthier Lifestyles?" *Psychological Science in the Public Interest* 4, no. 1 (2003): 1–44.

2. G. Barker and S. Graham, "Developmental Study of Praise and Blame as Attributional Cues," *Journal of Educational Psychology* 79, no. 1 (1987): 62–66.

3. Carol S. Dweck, "Messages That Motivate: How Praise Molds Students' Beliefs, Motivation, and Performance (in Surprising Ways)," in *Improving Academic Achievement: Impact of Psychological Factors on Education*, ed. J. Aronson (New York: Academic Press, 2002).

4. C. S. Dweck and M. L. Kamins, "Person Versus Process Praise and Criticism: Implications for Contingent Self-Worth and Coping," *Developmental Psychology* 35, no. 3 (1999): 835–47.

5. Ibid.

6. Ibid.

7. C. S. Dweck and C. M. Mueller, "Praise for Intelligence Can Undermine Children's Motivation and Performance," *Journal of Personality and Social Psychology* 75, no. 1 (1998): 33–52.

8. John M. Gottman, *The Marriage Clinic: A Scientifically-Based Marital Therapy* (New York: W. W. Norton, 1999).

9. Steven W. Kairys, et al., "The Psychological Maltreatment of Children— Technical Report," *Pediatrics* 109, no. 4 (2002): e68.

10. John Gottman, 1999, 191–93.

CHAPTER 10

1. S. S. Luthar and B. E. Becker, "Privileged but Pressured? A Study of Affluent Youth," *Child Development* 73, no. 5 (2002): 1593–610.

2. C. Schwartz, et al., "Altruistic Social Interest Behaviors Are Associated with Better Mental Health," *Psychosomatic Medicine* 65, no. 5 (2003): 778–85.

3. Demitri Papolos and Janice Papolos, *The Bipolar Child: The Definitive and Reassuring Guide to Childhood's Most Misunderstood Disorder* (New York: Broadway, 2002), 155.

4. Stephen R. Covey, *The 7 Habits of Highly Effective People* (New York: Simon and Schuster, 1989), 138.

5. Kennon M. Sheldon, et al., "What Is Satisfying About Satisfying Events? Testing 10 Candidate Psychological Needs," *Journal of Personality and Social Psychology* 80, no. 2 (2001): 325–39.

6. Stephen Reiss, "Secrets of Happiness," *Psychology Today*, January/February 2001.

7. L. C. Chang and R. M. Arkin, "Materialism as an Attempt to Cope with Uncertainty," *Psychology and Marketing* 9, no. 5 (2002): 389–406.

8. H. G. Koenig, "Religion, Spirituality and Medicine: Application to Clinical Practice," *Journal of the American Medical Association* 284, no. 13 (2000): 1708.

9. V. Ramachandran, "The Neural Basis of Religious Experience," paper delivered at the annual meeting for the Society for Neuroscience, October 1997.

10. Bjørn Grinde, "How Can Science Help Religion Towards Optimal Benefit for Society," *Zygon* (forthcoming, 2005), manuscript supplied by author.

11. Andrew Newburg, et al., *Why God Won't Go Away: Brain Science and the Biology of Belief* (New York: Ballantine Books, 2002).

12. V. A. Barnes, et al., "Impact of Transcendental Meditation on Ambulatory Blood Pressure in African-American Adolescents," *American Journal of Hypertension* 17, no. 4 (2004): 366–69.

13. Alicia Fortinberry, "Empower Your Body," audio CD (Nevada: Hopeline, 1998).

CHAPTER 11

1. N. S. Mauthner, "Postnatal Depression: The Significance of Social Contacts Between Mothers," *Women's Studies International Forum* 18, no. 3 (1995): 311–23.

2. Richard O'Connor, *Undoing Depression: What Therapy Doesn't Teach You and Medication Can't Give You* (New York: Berkeley, 1999), 250.

3. Ibid., 251.

4. C. Stanger, "Behavioral and Emotional Problems Among Children of Drug Abusers," *Psychiatric Times* 20, no. 2 (2003).

5. Edmund Leach, *The Listener*, 30 November 1967, 695.

6. Anthony Stevens and John Price, *Evolutionary Psychiatry*, 2d ed. (London: Routledge, 2000).

7. M. E. Pipe and J. C. Wilson, "Cues and Secrets: Influences on Children's Event Reports," *Developmental Psychology* 30, no. 4 (1994): 515–25.

8. Barry A. Farber, et al., "Clients' Perceptions of the Process and Consequences of Self-Disclosure in Psychotherapy," *Journal of Counseling Psychology* 51, no. 3 (2004): 340–46.

9. Bjørn Grinde, *Darwinian Happiness: Evolution as a Guide for Living and Understanding Human Behavior* (Princeton, NJ: Darwin Press, 2002); Anthony Stevens and John Price, 2000.

10. W. Van der Does, "Thought Suppression and Cognitive Vulnerability to Depression," *British Journal of Clinical Psychology* 44, no. 1 (2005): 1–14.

11. J. Crocker and L. E. Park, "The Costly Pursuit of Self-Esteem," *Psychological Bulletin* 130, no. 3 (2004): 392–414.

12. Ibid.

CHAPTER 12

1. J. H. Meyer, et al., "Dysfunctional Attitudes and 5-HT2 Receptors During Depression in Self-Harm," *American Journal of Psychiatry* 160, no. 1 (2003): 90–99.

2. Kristi L. Lockhart, et al., "Young Children's Beliefs About the Stability of Traits: Protective Optimism?" *Child Development* 73, no. 5 (2002): 1408–30.

3. Martin Seligman, *Learned Optimism: How to Change Your Mind and Your Life* (New York: Random House, 1991); Martin Seligman, *The Optimistic Child: Proven Program to Safeguard Children from Depression and Build Lifelong Resistance* (New York: Harper Perennial, 1996).

4. Martin Seligman, 1996, 14.

5. Martin Seligman, 1991, 44.

6. Robert Brooks and Sam Goldstein, *Raising Resilient Children: Fostering Strength, Hope, and Optimism in Your Child* (Lincolnwood, IL: Contemporary Books, 2001), 135.

7. Ibid., 13.

8. G. Ainslie and J. Monterosso, "A Marketplace in the Brain," *Science* 306, no. 5695 (2004): 421–23.

9. Angela Prencipe and Philip David Zelazo, "Development of Affective Decision-Making for Self and Other: Evidence for the Integration of First- and Third-Person Perspectives," *Psychological Science* 16, no. 7 (2005): 501–5.

CHAPTER 13

1. R. Birrer and S. Vemuri, "Depression in Later Life: A Diagnostic and Therapeutic Challenge," *American Family Physician* 69, no. 10 (2004): 2375–89.

2. National Institutes of Health, Consensus Development Conference Statement, "Diagnosis and Treatment of Attention-Deficit/Hyperactivity Disorder (ADHD)," *Journal of the American Academy of Child Adolescent Psychiatry* 39, no. 2 (2000): 182–93.

3. American Psychiatric Association, *Diagnostic and Statistical Manual of Mental Disorders*, 4th ed. (Washington, DC: American Psychiatric Association, 1994).

4. P. N. Pastor and C. A. Reuben, "Attention Deficit Disorder and Learning Disability: United States, 1997–98," National Center for Health Statistics, *Vital Health Stat* 10, no. 206 (2002).

5. Bjørn Grinde, *Darwinian Happiness: Evolution as a Guide for Living and Understanding Human Behavior* (Princeton, NJ: Darwin Press, 2002), 40–41, 118.

6. Bjørn Grinde, 2002.

7. R. D. Ladnier and A. E. Massanari, "Treating ADHD as Attachment Deficit Disorder," in *Handbook of Attachment Interventions*, ed. T. M. Levy (San Diego: Academic Press, 2000).

8. G. Halasz and A. Vance, "Attention Deficit and Hyperactivity Disorder in Children: Moving Forward with Divergent Perspectives," *Medical Journal of Australia* 177, no. 10 (2002): 554–57.

9. F. F. Ng, et al., "Children's Achievement Moderates the Effects of Mothers' Use of Control and Autonomy Support," *Child Development* 75, no. 3 (2004): 764–80.

10. I. Perner, et al., "Executive Control and Higher-Order Theory of Mind in Children at Risk of ADHD," *Infant and Child Development* 11, no. 2 (2002): 141–58.

11. D. Christakis, et al., "Early Television Exposure and Subsequent Attentional Problems in Children," *Pediatrics* 13, no. 4 (2004): 708–13.

12. L. Beseler, "Effects on Behavior and Cognition: Diet and Artificial Colors, Flavors, and Preservatives," *International Pediatrics* 14, no. 1 (1999): 41–43.

13. S. Kranz, et al., "Changes in Diet Quality of American Preschoolers Between 1977 and 1998," *American Journal of Public Health* 94, no. 9 (2004): 1525–30.

14. C. Hannaford, *Smart Moves: Why Learning Is Not All in Your Head* (Arlington, VA: Great Ocean Pub., 1995).

15. B. R. H. Van den Bergh and A. Marcoen, "High Antenatal Maternal Anxiety Is Related to ADHD Symptoms, Externalizing Problems, and Anxiety in 8- and 9-Year-Olds," *Child Development* 75, no. 4 (2004): 1085–97.

16. A. Pellegrini and P. Batchford, "The Developmental and Educational Significance of Recess in Schools," *Early Report* 29, no. 1 (2002): 1–7.

17. F. Kuo and A. Taylor, "A Potential Natural Treatment for Attention-Deficit/Hyperactivity Disorder: Evidence from a National Study," *American Journal of Public Health* 94, no. 9 (2004): 1580–86.
18. Sandra B. Barker, "Therapeutic Aspects of the Human–Companion Animal Interaction," *Psychiatric Times* 16, no. 2 (1999): 45–46. K. Allen, "Cardiovascular Reactivity and the Presence of Pets, Friends, and Spouses: The Truth About Cats and Dogs," *Psychosomatic Medicine* 64 (2002): 727–39.

CHAPTER 14

1. A. Troisi, et al., "Early Separation Anxiety and Adult Attachment Style in Women with Eating Disorders," *British Journal of Clinical Psychology* 44, no. 1 (2005): 89–97.
2. C. McNeely, et al., "Mothers' Influence on the Timing of First Sex Among 14- and 15-Year-Olds," *Journal of Adolescent Health* 31, no. 3 (2002): 256–65.
3. A. Troisi et al., 2005.
4. H. K. Dohnt and M. Tiggemann, "Peer Influences on Body Dissatisfaction and Dieting Awareness in Young Girls," *British Journal of Developmental Psychology* 23 (2005): 103–16.
5. D. L. Braun, et al., "Psychiatric Comorbidity in Patients with Eating Disorders," *Psychological Medicine* 24, no. 4 (1994): 859–67.
6. L. Smolak, et al., "Parental Input and Weight Concerns Among Elementary School Children," *International Journal of Eating Disorders* 25, no. 3 (1999): 263–71.
7. Eric Stice, et al., "Psychological and Behavioral Risk Factors for Obesity Onset in Adolescent Girls: A Prospective Study," *Journal of Consulting and Clinical Psychology* 73, no. 2 (2005): 195–202.
8. Michael McDowell, quoted by Julie Robotham in "Telly's Done a Bad Bad Thing," *Sydney Morning Herald*, 19 May 2004.
9. David Ludwig, et al., "Relation Between Consumption of Sugar-Sweetened Drinks and Childhood Obesity: A Prospective, Observational Analysis," *The Lancet* 357, no. 9255 (2001): 505–8.

10. M. J. Essex, et al., "Maternal Stress Beginning in Infancy May Sensitize Children to Later Stress Exposure: Effects on Cortisol and Behavior," *Biological Psychiatry* 52, no. 8 (2002): 774–84.

11. Hillary Burdette, quoted in "In TV Habits, Like Mother, Like Child," Eric Nagourney, *New York Times*, 16 October 2001.

12. Stacey Tantleff-Dunn, quoted in a press release "Ads with 'Supersized' Actors Leave Men Depressed, Unhappy with Their Muscles, UCF Study Shows," University of Central Florida, 5 May 2004.

13. Nancy M. Wells, "At Home with Nature: Effects of 'Greenness' on Children's Cognitive Functioning," *Environment and Behavior* 32, no. 6 (2000): 775–95; Rebecca A. Clay, "Green Is Good for You," *Monitor on Psychology* 32, no. 4 (2001): 40–42.

CHAPTER 15

1. June Price Tangney, "Constructive and Destructive Aspects of Shame and Guilt," in *Constructive and Destructive Behavior: Implications for Family, School, and Society*, ed. Arthur C. Bohart and Deborah J. Stipek (Washington, DC: American Psychological Association, 2001).

2. C. Zahn-Waxler, et al., "Patterns of Guilt in Children of Depressed and Well Mothers," *Developmental Psychology* 26, no. 1 (1990): 51–59.

3. S. C. Clarke, "Advance Report of Final Divorce Statistics, 1989 and 1990," *Monthly Vital Statistics Report* 43(9S) (Hyattsville, MD: National Center for Health Statistics, 1995).

4. E. Winslow, et al., "Preventive Interventions for Children of Divorce," *Psychiatric Times* 21, no. 2 (2004).

5. J. S. Tucker, et al., "Parental Divorce: Effects on Individual Behavior and Longevity," *Journal of Personality and Social Psychology* 73, no. 2 (1997): 381–91.

6. Thomas G. O'Connor, et al., "Are Associations Between Parental Divorce and Children's Adjustment Genetically Mediated? An Adoption Study," *Developmental Psychology* 36, no. 4 (2000): 429–37.

7. Frederick Rose, *The Traditional Mode of Production of the Australian Aborigines* (Sydney: Angus & Robertson, 1987).

8. Mika Kivimäki, et al., "Death or Illness of a Family Member, Violence, Interpersonal Conflict, and Financial Difficulties as Predictors of Sickness Absence: Longitudinal Cohort Study on Psychological and Behavioral Links," *Psychosomatic Medicine* 64, no. 5 (2002): 817–25.

9. O'Connor, et al., 2000.

10. I. N. Sandler, et al., "Coping Efficacy and Psychological Problems of Children of Divorce," *Childhood Development* 71, no. 4 (2000): 1099–118; S. A. Wolchik, et al., "Maternal Acceptance and Consistency of Discipline as Buffers of Divorce Stressors on Children's Psychological Adjustment Problems," *Journal of Abnormal Childhood Psychology* 28, no. 1 (2000): 87–102.

11. Robert Bauserman, "Child Adjustment in Joint-Custody Versus Sole-Custody Arrangements: A Meta-Analytic Review," *Journal of Family Psychology* 16, no. 1 (2002): 91–102.

12. Sanford L. Braver, et al., "Relocation of Children After Divorce and Children's Best Interests: New Evidence and Legal Considerations," *Journal of Family Psychology* 17, no. 2 (2003): 206–19.

13. Susan S. Bartell, "Birth of a Second Child: A Unique Impact on the Family System," *International Journal of Childbirth Education* 19, no. 3 (2004): 4–8.

14. Ibid.

15. R. A. Weller, et al., "Depression in Recently Bereaved Prepubertal Children," *American Journal of Psychiatry* 148, no. 11 (1991): 1536–40.

16. Cynthia R. Pfeffer, "Helping Children Cope with Death," *Psychiatric Times* 17, no. 9 (2000).

CHAPTER 16

1. James Q. Wilson, *The Marriage Problem: How Our Culture Has Weakened Families* (New York: Harper Collins, 2002).

2. Mary Bold, "Blended Families-2," Center for Parent Education, University of Texas, 2001, unt.edu/cpe/module1/blk2blend.htm.

3. B. Ram and F. Hou, "Changes in Family Structure and Child Outcomes: Roles of Economic and Familial Resources," *Policy Studies Journal* 31, no. 3 (2003): 309–30.

4. H. Ono, "Marital History Homogamy Between the Divorced and the Never Married Among Non-Hispanic Whites," *Social Science Research* 34, no. 2 (2005): 333–56.

5. R. D. Conger, et al., "Competence in Early Adult Romantic Relationships: A Developmental Perspective on Family Influences," *Prevention and Treatment* 4, no. 11 (2001).

6. A. Case and C. Paxson, "Mothers and Others: Who Invests in Children's Health?" (paper, Research Program in Development Studies, Princeton University, 2000).

7. U.S. Bureau of the Census, "Marital Status and Living Arrangements," *Current Population Reports*, Series P20-514 (Washington, DC: Government Printing Office, 1998).

8. D. C. Renshaw, "Fathering," *Psychiatric Times* 21, no. 11 (2004).

9. Ariel Kalil, et al., "Living Arrangements of Single-Mother Families: Variations, Transitions, and Child Development Outcomes" (Working Paper 01.20, Harris School, University of Chicago, September 2001).

10. C. R. Hess, et al., "Resilience Among African American Adolescent Mothers: Predictors of Positive Parenting in Early Infancy," *Journal of Pediatric Psychology* 27, no. 7 (2002): 619–29.

11. Susan L. Brown and Alan Booth, "Cohabitation Versus Marriage: A Comparison of Relationship Quality," *Journal of Marriage and the Family* 58 (1996): 668–78; R. K. Raley and E. Wildsmith, "Cohabitation and Children's Family Instability," *Journal of Marriage and Family* 66, no. 1 (2004): 210–19; D. Popenoe, *Life Without Father: Compelling New Evidence That Fatherhood and Marriage Are Indispensable for the Good of Children and Society* (New York: Free Press, 1996).

12. Jan E. Stets, "Cohabiting and Marital Aggression: The Role of Social Isolation," *Journal of Marriage and Family* 53 (1991): 669–80.

CHAPTER 17

1. John P. Murray, "TV Violence and Brainmapping in Children," *Psychiatric Times* 18, no. 10 (2001): 70–71; J. B. Funk, et al., "Violence Exposure in Real-Life, Video Games, Television, Movies, and the Internet: Is There Desensitization?" *Journal of Adolescence* 27, no. 1 (2004): 23–39.

2. C. A. Anderson and K. E. Dill, "Video Games and Aggressive Thoughts, Feelings, and Behavior in the Laboratory and in Life," *Journal of Personality and Social Psychology* 78, no. 4 (2000): 772–90.

3. T. N. Robinson, et al., "Effects of Reducing Children's Television and Video Game Use on Aggressive Behavior," *Archives of Pediatrics and Adolescent Medicine* 155, no. 1 (2001): 17–23.

4. A. Novac, "Traumatic Stress and Human Behavior," *Psychiatric Times* 18, no. 4 (2001): 41–43.

5. C. Oates, et al., "Children and Television Advertising: When Do They Understand Persuasive Intent?" *Journal of Consumer Behavior* 1, no. 3 (2002): 238–45.

6. Ibid.

7. M. Story and S. French, "Food Advertising and Marketing Directed at Children and Adolescents in the U.S.," *International Journal of Behavioral Nutrition and Physical Activity* 1, no. 3 (2004).

8. S. Lennon and J. H. Park, "Television Apparel Shopping: Impulse Buying and Parasocial Interaction," *Clothing and Textiles Research Journal* 22, no. 3 (2004): 135–44.

9. Donna L. Mumme and Anne Fernald, "The Infant as Onlooker: Learning from Emotional Reactions Observed in a Television Scenario," *Child Development* 74, no. 1 (2003): 221–37.

10. K. J. Pine and A. Nash, "Dear Santa: The Effects of Television Advertising on Young Children," *International Journal of Behavioral Development* 26, no. 6 (2002): 529–39.

11. For example, C. Hughes, et al., "Antisocial, Angry and Unsympathetic: 'Hard to Manage' Preschoolers' Peer Problems, and Possible Cognitive Influences," *Journal of Child Psychology and Psychiatry* 41, no. 2 (2000):

169–79; V. Stevens, et al., "Relationship of Family Environment in Children's Involvement in Bully-Victims Problems in School," *Journal of Youth and Adolescence* 31, no. 6 (2002): 419–28.

12. M. Mahady-Wilton, et al., "Emotional Regulation and Display in Classroom Victims of Bullying: Characteristic Expressions of Affect, Coping Styles and Relevant Contextual Factors," *Social Development* 9, no. 2 (2000): 226–45.

13. D. Wolke, et al., "Bullying Involvement in Primary School and Common Health Problems," *Archives of Diseases in Childhood* 85, no. 3 (2001): 197–201.

14. See J. B. Pearce and A. E. Thompson, "Practical Approaches to Reduce the Impact of Bullying," *Archives of Diseases in Childhood* 79, no. 6 (1998): 528–31.

15. P. Hawley, "Strategies of Control, Aggression, and Morality in Preschoolers: An Evolutionary Perspective," *Journal of Experimental Child Psychology* 85, no. 3 (2003): 215–35.

16. K. Rigby and P. T. Slee, "Bullying Among Australian School Children: Reported Behavior and Attitudes Toward Victims," *Journal of Social Psychology* 131, no. 5 (1991): 615–27.

17. M. J. Boulton, "Concurrent and Longitudinal Relations Between Children's Playground Behavior and Social Preference, Victimization, and Bullying," *Child Development* 70, no. 4 (1999): 944–54.

18. R. D. Duncan, "Peer and Sibling Aggression: An Investigation of Intra- and Extra-Familial Bullying," *Journal of Interpersonal Violence* 14, no. 8 (1999): 871–86.

19. F. Mishna, "A Qualitative Study of Bullying from Multiple Perspectives," *Children and Schools* 26, no. 4 (2004): 234–47.

20. R. Kaltialo-Heino, et al., "Bullying, Depression and Suicidal Ideation in Finnish Adolescents: School Survey," *British Medical Journal* 319, no. 7206 (1999): 348–51.

21. D. Schwartz, et al., "The Early Socialization of Aggressive Victims of Bullying," *Child Development* 68, no. 4 (1997): 665–75.

22. R. D. Duncan, 1999.

23. J. B. Pearce and A. E. Thompson, 1998.
24. Joan K. Peters, *When Mothers Work: Loving Our Children Without Sacrificing Ourselves* (Reading, MA: Perseus, 1998).
25. M. Eberstadt, *Home-Alone America: The Hidden Toll of Day Care, Behavioral Drugs and Other Parent Substitutes* (New York: Sentinel, 2004).
26. L. Ahnert, et al., "Transition to Child Care: Associations with Infant-Mother Attachment, Infant Negative Emotion, and Cortisol Elevations," *Child Development* 75, no. 3 (2004): 639–50.

BIBLIOGRAPHY

⊙

Belsky, J., et al., eds. *Child Care and Child Development: Results from the NICHD Study of Early Child Care and Youth Development.* New York: Guilford Press, 2005.

Bowlby, John. *The Making and Breaking of Affectional Bonds.* New York: Routledge, 1979.

Brooks, Robert, and Sam Goldstein. *Raising Resilient Children: Fostering Strength, Hope, and Optimism in Your Child.* Lincolnwood, IL: Contemporary Books, 2001.

Cortesi, David E. *Secular Wholeness: A Skeptic's Path to a Richer Life.* New Bern, NC: Trafford, 2002.

Dubovsky, Steven. *Mind-Body Deceptions: The Psychosomatics of Everyday Life.* New York: Norton & Co., 1997.

Eberstadt, M. *Home-Alone America: The Hidden Toll of Day Care, Behavioral Drugs and Other Parent Substitutes.* New York: Sentinel, 2004.

Fortinberry, Alicia. "Empower Your Body." Reno, NV: Hopeline, 1998. Audio CD.

Fraiberg, S. *The Magic Years.* New York: Scribner, 1959.

Goleman, Daniel. *Emotional Intelligence: Why It Can Matter More Than IQ.* London: Bloomsbury, 1996.

Gottman, John M. *The Marriage Clinic.* New York: W. W. Norton, 1999.

Grinde, Bjørn. *Darwinian Happiness: Evolution as a Guide for Living and Understanding Human Behavior.* Princeton, NJ: Darwin Press, 2002.

Jureidini, J., et al. "Efficacy and Safety of Antidepressants for Children and Adolescents," *British Medical Journal* 328 (2004): 879–83.

Karen, Robert. *Becoming Attached: First Relationships and How They Shape Our Capacity to Love.* New York: Oxford University Press, 1998.

Kimball, Jill, et al. *Drawing Families Together One Meal at a Time.* Orlando, FL: Active Media Pub, 2003.

Leach, P. *Your Baby and Child: From Birth to Age Five.* Rev. ed. New York: Knopf, 1997.

Lott, Deborah. "Brain Development, Attachment and Impact on Psychic Vulnerability." *Psychiatric Times* 15, no. 5 (1998): 1–5.

Moradi, S. Robert. "The Father-Child Connection: A Struggle of Contemporary Man." *Psychiatric Times* 14, no. 1 (1997).

Murray, Bob, and Alicia Fortinberry. *Creating Optimism: A Proven Seven-Step Program for Overcoming Depression.* Chicago: McGraw-Hill, 2004.

Nathanielsz, Peter W. *Life in the Womb: The Origin of Health and Disease.* Ithaca, NY: Promethean Press, 1999.

Newburg, Andrew, et al. *Why God Won't Go Away: Brain Science and the Biology of Belief.* New York: Ballantine Books, 2002.

O'Connor, Richard. *Undoing Depression: What Therapy Doesn't Teach You and Medication Can't Give You.* New York: Berkeley, 1999.

Popenoe, D. *Life Without Father: Compelling New Evidence That Fatherhood and Marriage Are Indispensable for the Good of Children and Society.* New York: Free Press, 1996.

Reiss, Stephen. "Secrets of Happiness." *Psychology Today*, January/February 2001.

Ridley, Matt. *Nature via Nurture: Genes, Experience and What Makes Us Human.* New York: HarperCollins, 2003.

———. *Origins of Virtue: Human Instincts and the Evolution of Cooperation.* New York: Penguin Viking, 1996.

Salk, Lee. *What Every Child Would Like His Parents to Know.* New York: Warner Books, 1973.

Schore, Allan N. *Affect Regulation and the Origin of the Self: The Neurobiology of Emotional Development.* Hillsdale, NJ: Lawrence Erlbaum, 1999.

Sears W., et al. *The Baby Book.* 2d ed. New York: Little Brown, 2003.

Seligman, Martin. *The Optimistic Child: Proven Program to Safeguard Children from Depression and Build Lifelong Resistance.* New York: Harper Perennial, 1996.

Siegel, Daniel J. *The Developing Mind: How Relationships and the Brain Interact to Shape Who We Are.* New York: Guilford Press, 2001.

Stevens, Anthony, and John Price. *Evolutionary Psychiatry.* 2d ed. London: Routledge, 2000.

Stroufe, L. A., et al. *Child Development: Its Nature and Course.* 2d ed. New York: McGraw-Hill, 1992.

Turnbull, Colin. *The Forest People.* London: Pimlico, 1993.

Viorst, Judith. *Necessary Losses.* New York: Fawcett, 1986.

Walsh, Froma. *Strengthening Family Resilience.* New York: Guilford Press, 1998.

Wilson, James Q. *The Marriage Problem: How Our Culture Has Weakened Families.* New York: Harper Collins, 2002.

Wright, Robert. "Evolution of Despair." *Time,* 28 August 1995.

INDEX

⊙

232

Index